# CAN'T WAIT TO COMMUNICATE:

## FROM BIRTH TO SIX

THERESA M. SULL, PH.D.

# DEDICATION

To my mother, Theresa C. Sudak,
who launched my communication skills with
unselfish devotion.

# ACKNOWLEDGEMENTS

Many researchers and theorists have inspired my writing, but any omissions or mistakes in CAN'T WAIT TO COMMUNICATE are my own. After years of research in libraries, I now conduct research at home on my Apple iMac. On my computer I can access internet sites like Alibris, Amazon, and Wikipedia. Armloads of library books could not provide as much information as I find with my fingertips today.

# ABOUT THE AUTHOR

Theresa M. Sull, Ph.D. earned her doctorate in *Educational Psychology* at the University of North Carolina in Chapel Hill. She received a master's degree in *Teaching Young Children with Special Needs* at Wheelock College in Boston. Dr. Sull's experience includes teaching children, parents and grandparents, college students, and directors of childcare centers. Theresa sees herself as a bridge connecting educational theory and research with the family homes and classrooms where children are learning as they play.

Theresa Sull, Ph.D. published twenty articles for teachers, four nonfiction books for adults on children's education, and three books for children. Dr. Sull lives in Hillsborough, NC, where she watches birds and other wildlife in her backyard on the Eno River.

ISBN Number:
Library of Congress Control Number:

# TABLE OF CONTENTS

# INTRODUCTION
## An Invitation to Celebrate Communication

Adults who care for children begin with high expectations for those children. Whether I ask groups of parents, grandparents, teachers or administrators, most will report similar dreams for the children in their care.

Adults want children to become responsible, to have healthy relationships, to hold positive values, and to experience enjoyment and satisfaction in life.

Communication skills are at the heart of these aspirations. Adults hope that all children will become excellent communicators. Grown-ups want children to experience clear communication whether they're listening, speaking, singing or signing.

Infants have inborn communication skills to express their basic needs. Cooing, fussing, and crying help infants survive. When adults listen to a baby's communication, they can learn if that baby is cold, hungry, lonely or over-stimulated.

Human language is the most complex communication in the world!

Noam Chomsky, linguist and philosopher, stated that 100,000 years ago, one person's mutation installed a language faculty in human beings. But Steven Pinker, a linguist and cognitive psychologist, emphasized that the faculty for language evolved gradually from precursors of language in nonhuman primates.

Scholars divide language into two complementary processes called Receptive and Expressive Language. Receptive Language includes people's understanding of facial expressions, body movements and positions, and progressively more complex oral language. Expressive Language is used by people to communicate with everyone around them.

As children try to express more complicated ideas than those springing from their instinct to survive, they begin to use recognizable words. Soon they use the rules of word order that govern languages in their community. In English, *I love you* is the correct word order. In French, Je vous aime, or *I you love* is grammatically correct.

Receptive and expressive language are bidirectional processes. Bidirectional means moving in two opposite directions, but with each process affecting the other. Receptive language is intertwined with expressive language.

Before children can become expressively effective speakers and writers, they must understand receptively what people mean by their facial expressions, their gestures and their sounds. Both receptive and expressive language skills will be important for mature communication competence.

Older children and young adults will need to communicate with their family and friends. Email, postcards, telephone calls and written letters will explain how these young people are doing as they explore new education and employment opportunities.

How will children become competent communicators? Because most children Can't Wait to Communicate, they will be adults' strong allies in the process of language learning. Supporting children's communication is a solid investment in the future!

Here are twenty-six INSIGHTS that help adults understand and support children's language development. These insights range in length from four points that describe how to talk to young children, to a five-page timetable describing children's development.

The complete list of insights below, labeled with alphabet letters from A to Z, indicates each insight's name and page number.

# INSIGHTS

# CHAPTER 1
# The Importance of Communication

Why are communication skills so important? How do babies learn to communicate? When do young children begin to speak or to use sign language? Should adults encourage babies and children to communicate? Or should children simply observe other people's communication? When can children be taught to read and write?

Do shy children or gregarious children have an advantage in language learning? Can children learn to talk by watching educational television programs, by listening to the radio, or by watching educational DVDs? Should children be punished for talking too loudly, or should they be rewarded for their attempts to speak up? Can children learn two languages at the same time?

Because adults want children to become lifelong communicators, parents and other teachers often have many questions about children's listening and speaking skills. Adults usually realize that language is a critical characteristic of human beings. They know that excellent communication offers infinite benefits to all people.

Although each child is unique, most children learn to communicate on a typical schedule. At the moment of birth, infants reach their first communication milestone with their lusty cries. Typical babies quickly reach several more developmental milestones.

---

| 1-MONTH MILESTONES | 4-MONTH MILESTONES |
|---|---|
| Infant's eyes focus together | Infant's eyes follow moving objects |
| Baby holds her/his head erect | Baby smiles when fondled |
| Fusses or cries if uncomfortable | Holds her/his head steady in midline |
| Coos and gurgles with pleasure | Hands come to midline of body |

---

Knowledgeable observers, such as physicians, nurses and teachers won't draw conclusions from a small samples of a child's behavior. They'll take notes on several observations over time. Professionals use assessment tools, such as the *Bracken Basic Concept Scale,* the *Kaufman Assessment Battery for Children,* and the *Preschool Language Scales.*

Both heredity and experience, or nature and nurture, affect the pace of children's development. Timelines of growth and the stages of communication development, can be found in doctor's offices, in textbooks, and at websites like *Wikipedia.*

No individual child's development follows these published timelines exactly. Each child is a unique individual who follows a unique course of development.

When adults help children communicate, supporting their efforts to draw or to talk, adults give children the gift of self-empowerment. Language lets children refine and report their innermost thoughts.

When children communicate, the caring people around them will listen with heightened focus and eagerly will respond. This reinforcement strengthens children's desire to communicate.

My daughter Linnet demonstrated self-empowerment when she was scribbling in her high chair. Linnet was using paper and crayons on her tray, staying safely away from my feet while I washed the dishes. She scribbled irregular circles, then she announced, "It's a person!"

I dated that paper to record Linnet's discovery of representation.

I don't think Linnet intentionally drew a person that day. Most children don't draw even a circle before they're three. But young children notice that their scribbles remind them of objects or people. This brings them a step closer to drawing what another person can recognize. A step closer to communication competence.

## Insights A: 6 Ways Communication Empowers

1. Communication Can Be Creative

2. Communication Promotes Logical Thought

3. Communication Leads to Reading and Writing

4. Communication Validates Identity

5. Communication Demonstrates Development

6. Communication Connects People

First, communication can be creative. Young children use language creatively as they individually discover the rules and conventions of their native language.

As children begin to talk, they demonstrate developmentally normal errors in language. For example, they often over-generalize concepts. Eleven-month-old Max was over-generalizing when he rubbed his friend's head and said "Ball!"

At that time, he used the word ball to refer to any curved object.

Two-year-old Julia moved toward a sliding glass door to pet an opossum on the deck. "Kitty!" she shouted, an over-generalization of the word kitty to mean any small furry animal. Adults know that opossum bites could cause rabies. But Julia didn't notice the red eyes and skinny tail that meant "Don't touch this wild animal!"

Before they're familiar with conventional expressions, children use language creatively to explain their experiences. As television entertainer Art Linkletter said, "Kids say the darndest things!"

Adults who live with children often hear humorous remarks. They might jot them in a baby book and send them to family or friends.

In church one Sunday, my little sister Linda asked me, "When are they going to sing Baa, Baa, Baa?" She was referring to Yale's Whiffenpoof Song, a drinking tune with lyrics including:

> We are poor little lambs
> Who have lost our way.
> Baa! Baa! Baa!
> We are little black sheep
> Who have gone astray.
> Baa! Baa! Baa!

Although Linda had heard this on a record by Bing Crosby, that particular song was not in the repertoire of the church choir!

As children grow, the adults around them remember children's creative expressions and repeat them. Children's language often amuses adults. For example, two-year-old Julia said "I puppying" whenever she was crawling on the floor, an expression that delighted everyone around her.

Other creative uses of early language are poignant or beautifully expressive. One child said that a teakettle was crying to be taken off the burner. Another said that deep snow was colding the ground. The famous painter Pablo Picasso said that he spent much of his adult life trying to draw like a child. In a similar way, writers must relearn children's creativity.

Many adults record evidence of their children's budding creativity. I filled drawers with my two daughters' early drawings and writings, and they loved seeing their childish work when they were older. When young children put their thoughts into words, they're already composing, although they still cannot write.

The Second way communication empowers is that communication promotes logical thought. As children speak, they clarify their thinking. Most children have parents, grandparents or teachers who will record children's early communication in writing.

Children's oral communication ability will develop before their abilities to read or to write. Talking is almost always a prerequisite to reading and writing. This is the Third way communication skills are empowering.

Many adults focus most on the development of children's reading skills. We live in an age when literacy is highly valued. Whether teaching young children to recite or to sing the alphabet, or teaching them to recognize their written names, grown-ups hope that this early rote learning will lead to better reading skills.

Most teachers of young children recognize the connections between early reading and early writing. Some understand the importance of oral and written communication, beyond skills like forming alphabet letters and numerals.

Literacy experts state that early reading and writing skills influence each other bidirectionally. Improved reading leads to better writing, and improved writing leads to better reading.

Bidirectional influences are especially evident in the early years, when the pleasure of language is new to children. Before children begin to read, they must understand seven concepts of literacy.

## Insights B: 7 Basic Concepts Of Literacy

1. Speech Can Be Written

2. What's Written Can Be Read

3. Most Adults Can Read

4. What's Read Can Be Spoken Aloud

5. Certain Combinations of Letters Are Words

6. Some Combinations of Words Are Sentences

7. In Sentences, Word Order Is Important

The Fourth way communication empowers is that communication validates children's identity. For example, identity is validated when children see their names written on packages from Grandma or other relatives. When they see labels on their clothing in school, the usefulness of reading and writing is evident.

Children can be taught to print their names on holiday cards for family and friends. Older preschoolers recognize their names on their cubbies and on charts in classrooms and childcare centers. Labels help children find their artwork, lunchboxes, or sweaters.

If a parent serves in the military, children can be uprooted. Often they can't build friendships before the next move. To reduce feelings of rootlessness, the military supports transients by moving most personal belongings, and hosting events to acquaint strangers.

Children can feel like outsiders in new schools and neighborhoods. They won't be comfortable until they feel that they belong in the new environment. Adults should support children's feelings of belongingness and relatedness. These emotions comfort children and contribute to their motivation for academic success.

The Fifth way communication empowers is that it demonstrates children's level of development. Communication gives parents and other teachers clues about children's current thinking. Concerns about a new sibling, or about Grandpa's illness, might emerge in children's behavior, in conversations, or in drawings and writing. An adult can learn about children's feelings and thoughts by paying close attention to their oral and written communication.

Like dancing, drawing, and other self-expression, speech and writing can be personally validating. A preschooler can say,

"I'm Amy. I'm three." A child can print her name on a greeting card. An older child can compose a poem for Mother's Day.

I can still recite a poem I wrote in the third grade. I thought it was an insightful statement about nature, but alas, I was not a budding Robert Frost. My childish poem did suggest that, in the future, I might write more meaningful words about the natural world.

# THE CARDINAL
## by Theresa, age 9

Red and black, and pretty indeed,
The cardinal comes down for a sunflower seed.
His crest stands quite high, and I love him so.
He flies kind of high, and he flies kind of low.

Although my interest in bird watching didn't take flight until I was in my forties, eventually I published several articles on that topic. And I bought binoculars to watch birds at the feeders on my deck.

Communicating in writing gave me an important power. There are no wrong ideas in personal communications.

Saying "Crackers crumble but they still taste good," is as correct as saying, "I hate the crumbly crackers we had for snack today." All children feel validated when their communications are accepted.

To elicit children's innermost thoughts, a teacher can ask a child to respond to a book that's read aloud. The ability to choose appropriate stories is an important skill for all teachers to master. Insights Q on page 68 lists fifty picture books to read to children in classrooms and homes.

After reading the book, *Alexander and the Terrible, Horrible, No Good, Very Bad Day* (1987) by Judith Viorst, adults can ask, "Have you ever felt sad like Alexander?" After reading *There's a Nightmare in My Closet* (1992) by Mercer Mayer, grown-ups can say "Tell me about your scary thoughts." In *Return to Augie Hobble* (2015) by Lane Smith, Augie works at an amusement park where a supernatural being might want to communicate with him.

Children's communication will demonstrate developing skills of language. Does the child who's learning English as a second language understand the use of plurals versus possessives? Can middle schoolers use one language at home and another language at school? Do older children know that nouns must agree with their antecedents to ensure clarity in their writing?

Good speakers and writers earn better grades in school. Eventually, students' college application essays will help them win college acceptance, and maybe win a scholarship. A polished interview and a well-written resume will help applicants get a job.

Many jobs require oral communication, written memos and reports. Today's professionals, including cashiers, doctors, lawyers, and restaurant workers, all need strong communication skills. Careers that require good writing increased with blogs and email.

Good relationships with neighbors are maintained through good communication. Talking to a contractor about remodeling needs, or telling a doctor about the symptoms of illness, require equally strong skills of oral communication.

My daughter Julia is a manager at the Hillsborough Yarn Shop. She uses her communication skills to sell yarn and pattern books, to post knitting and crocheting patterns, to maintain the shop's blog and website, and to teach a variety of classes.

I'm a list maker and use written lists to help make everyday decisions. I use daily To-Do lists to help me organize tasks, and use shopping lists to jog my memory. I use a journal to record my thoughts, and give this some credit for my mental health.

The Sixth and final way that communication empowers is that it connects people over space and time. Children's abilities to compose, draw, sign, sing, talk and write will give them ways to communicate with colleagues, family, friends, and others.

Blogs, emails, love letters, memos, telephone calls, thank-you notes, tweets and websites all rely on people's communication skills. Worthwhile human relationships require communication competence.

Many theorists of education, including those listed below in Insights C, emphasize the positive effects of human relationships on children's development. Communication skills foster good relationships, and good relationships are crucial to a satisfying life.

Using effective communication is as important in employment, as in friendships, as in marriages.

Educational researchers found that children who experienced secure attachment relationships in infancy become preschoolers with better social and pre-academic skills. Well-attached preschoolers have higher self-esteem and greater self-reliance than poorly attached peers.

Children's healthy interest in school starts with good relationships at home. The effects of early relationships with caretakers, parents and siblings will endure. Well-attached children co-operate in the required activities that promote learning in school.

Children who have more friends when they enter kindergarten will demonstrate more academic readiness than other schoolchildren. Then, if relationships are fostered in the classroom, children will make new friends, continue to enjoy school and to do well.

## Insights C: 14 Theorists Highlight Relationships

1. Vygotsky (1929) *Zone of Proximal Development*

2. Parten (1936) *Stages of Play*

3. Bowlby (1951) *Role of Responsive Care*

4. Erikson (1959) *Stage of Trust versus Mistrust*

5. McClelland (1961) *Motive of Affiliation*

6. Piaget (1965) *Importance of Peer Interaction*

7. Maslow (1968) *Need for Belongingness*

8. Tajfel (1971) *Social Identity*

9. Bandura (1977) *Role of Modeling and Imitation*

10. Deci and Ryan (1985) *Need for Relatedness*

11. Maxwell (2004) *Relationships 101*

12. Miller (2011) *Intimate Relationships*

13. Waldron and Kassing (2017) *Negotiating Workplace Relationships*

14. Ruiz and Amara (2018) *Seven Secrets to Healthy, Happy Relationships*

Parents and teachers can support children's friendships in the certainty that these relationships will help rather than hinder children's education. Researchers learned that children with healthy relationships in early childhood are likely to succeed in elementary school, in middle school, in high school and in college. In fact, such relationships can endure throughout life.

Children with higher communication skills will be more comfortable playing with other children than those who don't communicate well. Older students can send emails, letters or text messages to friends in town or in other states, as a way to maintain both near and long-distance relationships.

Children with Communication Competence send birthday letters, holiday cards, and thank-you notes to relatives. They read and write poetry, exploring the cadence of language. Later they write essays that impress college recruiters and win scholarships or internships with professionals.

If their relationships are supported, children demonstrate higher levels of communication competence as they mature. The twelve resources listed below provide information to help adults support children's learning.

# Insights D: 12 Resources For Parents And Teachers

1. *Childcraft: Poems of Early Childhood* (1949) by Field Enterprises

2. *The Magic Years: Understanding and Handling the Problems of Early Childhood* (1959) by Selma Fraiberg

3. *Infants and Mothers: Differences in Development* (1969) by T. Berry Brazelton

4. *Toddlers and Parents: A Declaration of Independence* (1974) by T. Berry Brazelton

5. *The Very Young: Guiding Children from Infancy Through the Early Years* (1993) by George W. Maxim

6. *Children's Thinking* (2004) by Martha Alibali and Robert Siegle

7. *The Read-Aloud Handbook: Sixth Edition* (2006) by Jim Trelease

8. *Diversity in Early Care and Education: Honoring Differences* (2007) by Janet Gonzalez-Mena

9. *The Whole-Brain Child: 12 Revolutionary Strategies to Nurture Your Child's Developing Mind* (2011) by Daniel J. Siegel, MD

10. *Raise Creative Thinkers: A Guide to Developing Children's Creative Intelligence* (2014) by Jackie McCarthy

11. *Child Development: 7th Edition* (2015) by Robert S. Feldman

12. *Yardsticks: Child and Adolescent Development Ages 4-14* (2018) by Chip Wood

Poetry's rhymes and rhythms draw children into language learning, introducing new vocabulary through context clues. Good resources include *Poems for Children: A Delightful Collection for Boys and Girls* (1993) compiled by Kate James and illustrated with paintings by Jessie Willcox Smith, M. E. Gray, and other impressive artists.

Poetry captured me in the 1949 edition of *Childcraft: Poems of Early Childhood.* To my daughters I read *Best Loved Nursery Rhymes and Songs* (1974), by Parents' Magazine Enterprises. *The Random House Book of Poetry for Children,* collected in 1983 by Jack Prelutsky, was illustrated by Arnold Lobel. Several books of poetry published after 2000 are listed below.

*Classic Poetry for Children* by Nicola Baxter came out in 2000. *A Family of Poems: My Favorite Poetry for Children* (2005) was compiled by Caroline Kennedy. *One Hundred Years of Poetry for Children,* edited by Michael Harrison, was published in 2007. *Small Worlds, of Bees and Trees and Butterfly Knees, a Book of Classic Poetry for Children: Nature with a Touch of Whimsy* by Tj Denby, Robert Louis Stevenson and Emily Dickenson came out in 2014. *The Sky Is for Wonder: Poetry for Children* by Ronnie Smith was published in 2015. *The Cambridge Book of Poetry for Children* by Kenneth Grahame was printed in 2018.

Theorists of development and classroom teachers have long recognized that children's relationships affect their communication ability and academic learning. Insights C on page 10 lists fourteen theorists who highlight the importance of relationships. From birth, children possess a powerful motivation for relatedness.

Ken Burns produced a documentary based on the letters of American Civil War soldiers. Many of those writers were only in their teens. Anne Frank was also a young teenager when she wrote about World War II in her famous diary.

There's just one more reason to emphasize communication competence. The *National Commission on Writing in America's Schools and Colleges* issued a ground-breaking report in 2003. The Commission reported that many students finish high school without the ability to write accurately and engagingly. This pioneering study is still cited in current articles about the importance of learning to write well.

How can adults ensure that all children are offered literacy's empowering gifts? What experiences that promote literacy will work for children at different ages? Which recommended activities don't really help children's language learning?

# CHAPTER 2
# Communication for Infants: Birth to 1 Year

It seems silly to be thinking about how good a communicator a baby might become, but the foundations of communication competence are laid in infancy. No, it's not necessary or even desirable to prop a baby in front of a television screen or a computer monitor. While computer skills are very valuable to young writers, they're not high on a list of communication basics.

If you have a new baby in the family, or if you're caring for babies in the nursery at a hospital or a childcare center, it's not too early to think about their growing communication competence. How can adults help these smallest children to gain the listening, speaking, reading and writing skills they'll need when they're older?

Long before children can write, they can put their thoughts into words to be recorded in writing by their caretakers. Some of these words should be sent to relatives in greeting cards.

Young children are developing Expressive Language, or the ability to use words to express meaning. Before infants can organize their thoughts into expressive language, however, they will need Receptive Language.

Newborns have very few language skills, but gradually they understand the spoken words of those who talk to them. Almost all infants are surrounded by a Language Envelope, an atmosphere as ordinary as the air they breathe. Insights H on page 23 describes in detail the Components of a Language-Rich Environment.

Children hear oral language from the people around them, and hear language on the radio and on television programs. They see written language on street signs and on billboards that advertise products from can openers, to cars, to cruises.

All oral language has value, but research suggests that the most influential language is the responsive language of the caregivers who interact directly with children. Responsive Language facilitates Receptive Language.

In about a year, by imitating the adults around them, most children will begin to express themselves in words, but their receptive language has been developing even before birth. Many newborns already recognize their mothers' inflections.

These infants heard their mothers' voices while they were still in the womb. Twenty-four weeks into a pregnancy, the fetus is sensitive to sounds coming from outside the mother's body.

People are primed to learn language because evolution made them language users. In *The Mother Tongue: English and How It Got That Way* (1990), author Bill Bryson reports one-month-old babies prefer speech sounds to any other sounds. Maybe these could be bird song, lawn motors, music, rain or wind chimes.

Scholars demonstrate how children the world over acquire language in a similar order at similar ages. Insights E on page 18 lists the communication skills attained at each age.

Adults can learn about children's development from a pediatrician, a teacher, or textbooks on human development. Because each child is unique, all children will not reach these milestones at the expected ages. Both nature, or what a child inherits, and nurture, or how a child is raised, affect the timetable of development.

Most children have typical personal timetables and a few children have atypical schedules. My older daughter Linnet was physically active, walking at ten months. My younger daughter Julia was physically cautious, but verbally precocious, talking at ten months.

A timeline of typical development can provide an approximation of children's changes as they grow and learn. No child's growth will follow a published timeline exactly, because each child is a unique individual.

If you're concerned about the rate or quality of your child's development, you can request a screening from specialists at your local public school system.

Psychologists will administer assessment instruments like the *Brigance Diagnostic Inventory of Early Development*, the *Kaufman Survey of Early Academic and Language Skills*, and the *McCarthy Scales of Children's Abilities*.

Insights E on page 18 describes the details of physical and communication development. Insights F on page 21 lists the six principles of development. Insights G on page 31 provides an overview of development in the physical, cognitive, emotional and social domains.

# Insights E: Physical & Communication Development

INFANT'S AGE   SKILLS ATTAINED

Newborn

Apgar Scores of 7 and over indicate normal activity, complexion, pulse, respiration and responsiveness.
Will cry if nose and mouth clear of mucous.

1 month

When upright, infant holds head erect.
Fusses or cries when uncomfortable.
Coos and gurgles with pleasure.

4 months

Eyes follow a moving person or object.
Coos or smiles if fondled.
Makes purposeful eye contact.
Can sit if body is supported.
Holds head steady in midline of body.

6 months

Reaches for an object in view.
Sits briefly while leaning on her/his arms.
Imitates adults' facial expressions.

7 months

Responds to her/his name.
Waves *bye-bye;* Shakes head *no;* Nods *yes.*
Sits unsupported for several minutes.

8 months

Babbles using several consonant sounds.
Creeps on belly and crawls.
Pulls to stand to see and reach objects.

9 months

Attends to familiar words.
Squeezes a squeaky toy in her/his hands.
Both eyes track her/his hands.

| 10 months | Imitates adult inflections; Babbles *gibberish*.<br>Says first recognizable word. |
|---|---|
| 12 months | Holds crayons in fist; Makes random marks.<br>Says three words beyond *Mama* and *Dada*.<br>Points to objects, people if asked *Where is…* |

**CHILD'S AGE:   SKILLS ATTAINED**

| 18 months | Points to simple pictures like *cat, dog, fish*.<br>Begins *pretend play*.<br>Scribbles with crayons, pencils, markers.<br>Refers to own self by name ("Mary eat").<br>Understands 10 times more than she says. |
|---|---|
| 2 years | Throws toys and tracks them visually.<br>Strings beads of one-inch diameter.<br>Holds crayons in fingers, not fist.<br>Has a vocabulary of 200 to 300 words.<br>Says 2-word phrases.<br>Refers to people with pronouns *he, me, she*. |
| 3 years | Strings beads of a half-inch diameter.<br>Makes pancakes, snakes, and balls of dough.<br>Imitates drawings of a *circle* and a *cross*<br>Has a vocabulary of 900 to 1,000 words.<br>Uses 3-word sentences. |
| 4 years | Moves body parts to a rhythmic beat.<br>Traces vertical lines, then horizontal lines.<br>Imitates drawing of a *square*.<br>Draws a person with 2 body parts.<br>Names random objects made of dough. |

Uses sentences averaging 4 to 4.5 words.
Has a vocabulary of 1,500 to 2,500 words.
Uses prepositions *above, behind, below*

5 years

Makes recognizable object of dough or clay.
Can hold a pencil correctly when shown.
Can trace letters and simple shapes.
Draws a person with 3 to 4 body parts.
Understands 4,000 to 5,000 words.
Uses sentences averaging 5 to 6 words.
Initiates conversations, even with strangers.
Tells imaginative stories.

6 years

Makes good eye contact.
Follows 2 to 3 step directions.
Draws a person with 5 to 7 body parts.
Copies first and last name.
Understands 20,000 to 24,000 words.
Has a vocabulary of 3,000 to 10,000 words.
Learns 5 to 10 new words a day.
Uses sentences averaging 6 to 7 words.
Uses *past, present,* and *future* tenses.
Reads common signs like EXIT and STOP.
Keeps time with rhythm instruments.

Experts in child development can determine whether a child is developing well, or whether he or she needs early intervention.

Six principles of development that help people appreciate children's progress are listed in Insights F, below. To get a complete picture of a child's progress, specialists will examine all domains listed in Insights G on page 21.

Physicians, and many experienced parents and other teachers, know that a child who sits or walks early won't necessarily talk early. Both gifted and disabled children can demonstrate uneven development.

## Insights F: Six Principles of Development

1.  Children develop differently in different environments

2.  Children develop at different rates in different Domains

3.  There are typical sequential steps in development

4.  Developmental stages are loosely tied to age

5.  Development in one area affects development in others

6.  Children's behaviors often reflect children's needs

## Insights G: Overview of Development: Three Domains

PHYSICAL DOMAIN
Sensory Perception: Processing information through all the senses
Gross Motor Skills: Large muscle movements of arms, legs, trunk
Fine Motor Skills: Small movements of eyes, fingers, mouth

COGNITIVE DOMAIN
Cognitive Skills: Intellectual, problem solving, or thinking skills
Language Skills: Receptive and Expressive skills

EMOTIONAL AND SOCIAL DOMAIN
Emotional (Affective) Skills: Expressing feelings of self and others
Social Skills: Interaction and relationships with people

# LANGUAGE DEVELOPMENT

The nativist account of language acquisition was proposed by Noam Chomsky. Chomsky was born in 1928 in Philadelphia, PA. His theoretical linguistic work from the 1950s revolutionized the field of linguistics. He treated language as a uniquely human, biologically based capacity. Affecting cognitive psychology and the philosophies of mind and language, Noam Chomsky helped initiate and sustain the cognitive revolution.

According to prominent theorist Jerome Bruner, infants and young children need extensive caregiver interaction to develop optimal language skills. In 1972, Bruner was appointed Watts Professor of Experimental Psychology at the University of Oxford. In his Oxford years, Bruner focused on early language development.

Rejecting the nativist account of language acquisition proposed by Noam Chomsky, Bruner offered an alternative in the form of an interactionist view of language development. In this approach, the social and interpersonal nature of language was emphasized.

Following Lev Vygotsky, the Russian theoretician of socio-cultural development, Jerome Bruner proposed that social interaction plays a significant role in the development of cognition. Bruner emphasized that children learn language in order to communicate. At the same time, they also learn the linguistic code.

Meaningful language is learned in the context of parent-infant interaction. Learning is scaffolded or supported by the child's Language Acquisition Support System.

The results of research into linguistics suggest that the known languages all over the world follow the same five rule systems listed below.

PHONOLOGY     (specific sounds used in language)
MORPHOLOGY   (how sounds in an order create words)
SYNTAX         (the order of words required by grammar)
SEMANTICS     (meanings carried by sentences)
PRAGMATICS    (uses of language in social situations)

Children eventually will use language as a system of symbols for communication. Their language can be oral, written, signed, and sung. Facility with language is a hallmark of being human.

Some animals respond to sounds of alarm or food calls made by other animals. But even chimpanzees, the great apes most closely related to human beings, have a very small capacity for symbolic representation, and an extremely limited ability to use language.

Because the early childhood years from birth through six are so important for language learning, parents and other teachers will provide activities to address all five rule systems listed above.

Insights H, below, describes a language-rich environment. Classroom teachers and parents at home will find lots of ideas in this list to enrich every child's language learning.

## Insights H: Components Of A Language-Rich Environment

MUSIC AND MOVEMENT

Sing traditional songs, including:

> Folk songs (*This train is bound for glory*)
> Camp songs (*There were ten in a bed… Roll over*)
> Holiday songs (*Jingle Bells, Peter Cottontail, Oh Chanukah*)
> Action songs (*If you're happy and you know it, clap your…*)

Sing about activities (*Take a little nap... Close your tired eyes*)
Have children dance or perform to the words of many songs.
Have children paint pictures to illustrate songs, poems and stories.

POETRY

Chant finger plays (*Here is the church, Here is the steeple*)
Recite poems (*Misty, Moisty Morning; Mix a Pancake*)
Read poetry (by Margaret Wise Brown, Shel Silverstein, ...)

LISTENING, TALKING, READING

Create a Language Envelope: Speak warmly, making eye contact.
Read many appropriate books to children.
Be a language model for children when talking to other adults.
Talk about visual displays like photos or pictures from magazines.
Display and talk about children's drawings and other art projects.
Label objects in classrooms and at home, often changing the labels.
Read aloud environmental print like street signs or advertisements.
Play rhyming games, word games and board games with children.
To encourage listening, make stuffed animals talk to children.
Take dictation to record children's ideas or stories.
Read the children's words back to them.
Use tape recorders so children can listen to themselves speak.
Use books on tape that children can follow in print.
Ask children open-ended questions: *Tell me about ...*
Be an active and reflective listener for children.
Give specific compliments: *You put on your shirt by yourself.*
Encourage children to talk to others: *Tell Dad about ...*
Have children tell stories and describe events from memory.

## EXPRESSIVE LANGUAGE

Expressive Language appears when babies become toddlers, at 12 or
18 months. Before adults hear children's first words, however, their

Receptive Language has been developing for about a year. Even so, it's a significant communication milestone when a baby says her first real words, which will be easily pronounced words like *Mama, Dada, baba* (bottle), *baby, ball, doggy, duck,* etc.

It's normal for children to speak at 10 months or at 18 months. My daughters were at opposite ends of this normal range. Linnet was the talky toddler and Julia the quiet one, but they both became very competent communicators.

How should caregivers create a supportive environment for language development? Special talking toys? Computer programs?

Educational research shows that infants need something much more simple than such gadgets. If used wisely, technology won't hurt a child's language development, but face-to-face contact is most important. The language parents and caregivers should use is called Better Baby Talk.

When adults speak Better Baby Talk, they facilitate better language skills, preparing infants to become great listeners and speakers. Baby Talk has a bad reputation. Certainly, "goo-goo, gaa-gaa" won't impress a knowledgable parent or a teacher.

Using real words and short sentences with babies will facilitate language development. Most grown-ups know intuitively that when they talk to babies they should start with face-to-face and eye-to-eye contact. They should bend down to the child's level and widen their eyes.

What can adults talk about to infants? During daily routines like bathing, dressing and feeding, adults should describe and explain their ongoing actions. They will use children's names when they speak to them. Responding to children's actions is key. Grown-ups should connect their words to the babies' reality.

"There's nice warm milk in this bottle. You're hungry!"
"The applesauce on the spoon feels cold, doesn't it?"
"What a soft washcloth! Let me wipe your mouth."
"Stretch out your legs! Here come your pajamas!"

Infants can't verbalize their interests, so adults need to hone their skills of observation to understand them. Babies indicate their interests with their raised arms or gazes. When adults verbalize babies' communication, they're teaching them words the children themselves soon will use to express their needs.

The rotating displays on the walls of children's rooms must appeal to the adults who carry babies around the room, as well as to the children themselves. Caregivers can talk about interesting pictures of animals, buildings, cars, clothes, furniture, people, and plants.

Photos of model rooms cut from magazines will inspire more comments from adults than a picture of Humpty Dumpty.

"This band and new vocalist sound great, and they're in town!"
"I am not voting for that man again! All our streets have potholes."
"This long dress on sale would work for New Year's Eve, no?"
"Maybe we'd like a little dog like this one someday."

The amount of speech that babies hear makes a big difference to them. Catch the baby's eyes before you begin to speak. Although children with disabilities like Autism avoid eye contact, most babies are drawn to people's flashing eyes. Infants tend to focus on any contrast between light and dark.

If you tip your face toward a baby while you raise your eyebrows, you'll display more white around the iris, making eyes more interesting. Cock your head to make your eyes even more obvious.

Researcher T. Berry Brazelton demonstrated that infants pay close attention to caregivers' facial expressions. For example, if adults stick out their tongues, infants often imitate them.

A baby's responsiveness is rewarding to grown-ups, who will be inspired to engage in more interactions. Babies respond more to higher-pitched voices, an evolutionary advantage because mothers were critical to survival. If overwhelmed, the babies will remove their attention.

Insights I provides four simple rules to help caregivers check their tone of voice to become better language models. By following these four rules, adults make language more attractive to infants, setting the stage for optimal language learning.

## Insights I: Tone Of Voice For Caregivers

USUALLY        (use accepting, calm and unemotional tones)
OFTEN          (use awed, enthusiastic and happy tones)
RARELY         (use cross, excited or loud tones)
NEVER          (use cold, frightening or hostile tones)

Because babies can't verbalize their interests, adults need to hone their skills of observation to understand babies. When adults express what babies might mean, they're teaching them the very words that the children will use later to make their needs known.

> "I see you want the teddy bear you dropped. Here it is."
> "You're looking at my shiny necklace, aren't you?"
> "I hear the telephone, too. Such a loud ring!"
> "That clock tells me that Dad will be home very soon."

Soon the babies themselves will begin to point out interesting objects. That is the beginning of a natural Sign Language. Babies' gestures can be enhanced by words learned in American Sign Language, or AMSLAN.

The *Signed English Dictionary for Preschool and Elementary Levels* (1975) by H. Bornstein, L. Tom, and N. Lundborg is a great resource for parents and other teachers of young children.

*Learn to Sign with Olli: The Fun Way to Learn Sign Language* (2007) by Garry Slack, features the monkey Olli to introduce signing to youngsters. *Fostering Communications with Young Children: Signing Fundamentals* (2015) by Lillian I. Hubler covers signing for children from birth to five years.

Interpreting a baby's cries takes attention and practice. But even if adults can't understand what the baby is expressing by fussing or crying, they can verbalize any discomfort they think the baby might be feeling. Soon young children will begin to express their own needs in words, based on language examples of caregivers.

> "Such loud crying! I can tell you're hungry."
> "That wet diaper must feel cold. No wonder you're fussy!"
> "Are you chilly? You might feel better when I wrap you up."
> "Let me sing you to sleep. I think you're feeling tired."

Singing lullabies to babies can sooth them to sleep, especially if they are danced slowly around a room. But songs also promote language development.

The rising and falling pitch of a melody is pleasant, and changes in pitch draw attention to words of a song.

Caregivers can sing traditional tunes, such as lullabies and folk songs, or they can make up new songs to sing about routines. To the melody of *Row, Row Your Boat*, parents could sing:

> Wash, wash, wash your hands (feet, etc.); Early in the da-ay.
> Down the drain with lots of splashes; Germs will go away.

Clean, clean, clean yourself, with water and with so-ap.
Freshen up in sink or tub; You're cute as one could hope.

If rhymes are spoken or sung, whether in nursery rhymes or in more sophisticated poetry, rhymes are another attention-getting strategy that promotes language learning. Rhymes are a mnemonic device, which means rhymes make language easier to remember.

Rhymes draw attention to grammar and also build vocabulary. Caregivers could invent rhymes to use during daily routines.

"Breakfast's over; we just ate. My banana tasted great."
"Have a green bean on a spoon. Lunch is coming very soon!"
"Baby's milk in baby's cup; Baby drinks her milk all up!"
"Sleepy time is almost here; Lullabies we'll want to hear."

Jean Piaget, 20th century Swiss theorist of Cognitive Development, emphasized the importance of young children's experiences with the physical world around them. As long as something is safe to play with (without sharp edges, small parts, or toxic paint) infants can play with any light-weight object.

The adults around the babies should comment on the things babies touch. This activity develops children's language skills. Physical manipulation and discussion of interesting objects encourage the babies' receptive and expressive skills.

Babies who cannot crawl need assistance from bigger people to reach play areas and toys. Adults around them help babies learn by creating play spaces on clean carpets or on sturdy blankets.

Although rattles and other plastic or wooden items are sold as toys, many things around the house lend themselves to babies' play. These everyday objects will be great toys for young children. Cloth napkins or wash cloths, plastic cups, measuring cups and spoons, empty yogurt and juice containers, all deserve mention.

"See the picture of red strawberries on this yogurt carton?"
"Here's the biggest measuring cup. I'll put it on the bottom."
"Let's put your baby doll to sleep under this dishtowel."

It's never too early to talk to babies, and it's never too early to read to them! From birth, a fussy infant can be soothed by the sound of a gentle voice reading aloud. Even a college textbook, a movie magazine, or the weekly newspaper can be read aloud to newborns.

Any material that interests adults will work, but grown-ups should dip into books of traditional nursery rhymes, too.

Insights J on page 31 lists sixteen nursery rhymes that have been recited for hundreds of years in English-speaking countries. Many more nursery rhymes can be found in the following volumes.

*Beatrix Potter's Nursery Rhyme Book* (2000) by Beatrix Potter

*The Big Book of Nursery Rhymes and Children's Songs* (2004)
    by Hal Leonard Corporation

*Favorite Nursery Rhymes from Mother Goose* (2007)
    by Scott Gustafson

*101 Nursery Rhymes & Sing-Along Songs for Kids* (2013)
    by Jennifer M. Edwards

*A Children's Treasury of Mother Goose* (2015) illustrated
    by Linda Bleck

*The Classic Mother Goose Nursery Rhymes: Over 101 Cherished
    Poems* (2018) by Gina Baek

# Insights J: Sixteen Nursery Rhymes To Recite

## THIS LITTLE PIGGY

This little piggy went to market,
This little piggy stayed home,
This little piggy had dumplings,
This little piggy had none.
And this little piggy cried,
"Wee, Wee, Wee, Wee..."
All the way home!

(Pull baby's fingers one by one)

## THE LITTLE MOUSE

Round and round,
Goes the little mouse.
Up the stairs, and into the house!

(1 finger circles hand, 2 fingers run up arm)

## LITTLE ARABELLA MILLER

Little Arabella Miller,
Caught a wooly caterpillar.
First it crawled upon her mother,
Then upon her baby brother.
They said, "Arabella Miller,
Take away this caterpillar!"

(Two fingers crawl up each arm)

## PAT-A-CAKE

Pat-a-cake, Pat-a-cake,
Baker's man,
Bake me a cake,
As fast as you can.
Roll it and pat it and mark it with a B,
And put it in the oven for baby and me!

(Give claps, pokes, rolling motions.)

## WEE WILLIE WINKIE

Wee Willie Winkie
Runs through the town,
Upstairs and downstairs,
In his dressing gown.
Rapping at the window,
Crying through the lock,
"Are the children in their beds,
Now it's nine o'clock?"

(Make knocking sounds as Willie raps)

## CHIN CHOPPER

Eye winker, eye blinker,
Nose smeller, mouth eater.
Chin chopper, chin chopper,
Chin chopper, chopper chin.

(Point to body part as mentioned)

## HICKORY, DICKORY DOCK

Hickory, Dickory, Dock!
The mouse ran up the clock.
The clock struck one,
The mouse ran down,
Hickory, Dickory, Dock!

(Fingers run up & down child's arms)

## LITTLE BOY BLUE

Little boy blue,
Come blow your horn,
The sheep's in the meadow,
The cow's in the corn.
Where is the boy
Who looks after the sheep?
He's under the haystack,
Fast asleep.

(Clasped hands around your mouth.)

## HEY DIDDLE DIDDLE

Hey, Diddle, Diddle,
The cat and the fiddle,
The cow jumped over the moon.
The little dog laughed,
To see such a sport,
And the dish ran away with the spoon!

(Pretend to play a fiddle.)

## TWINKLE TWINKLE LITTLE STAR

Twinkle, twinkle, little star,
How I wonder what you are.
Up above the world so high,
Like a diamond in the sky.
Twinkle, twinkle, little star,
How I wonder what you are.

(Point to the sky.)

## RIDE A COCK-HORSE

Ride a Cock-Horse to Banbury Cross,
To see a fine lady upon a white horse.
With rings on her fingers,
And bells on her toes,
She shall have music,
Wherever she goes.

(Child rides on adult's legs)

## BAA, BAA, BLACK SHEEP

Baa, Baa, Black Sheep, have you any wool?
Yes sir, yes sir, three bags full!
One for my master, and one for my dame,
And one for the little boy (girl), who lives down the lane!
Baa, Baa, Black Sheep, have you any wool?
Yes sir, yes sir, three bags full!

## ITSY BITSY SPIDER

The itsy bitsy spider
Went up the water spout,
Down came the rain
And washed the spider out.
Out came the sun
And dried up all the rain.
Now the itsy bitsy spider
Went up the spout again.

## ONE, TWO, BUCKLE MY SHOE

One, Two, buckle my shoe,
Three, Four, shut the door,
Five, Six, pick up sticks,
Seven, Eight, lay them straight,
Nine, Ten, a good fat hen,
Eleven, Twelve, dig and delve,
Thirteen, Fourteen, maids a-courting,
Fifteen, Sixteen, maids in kitchen,
Seventeen, Eighteen, maids in waiting,
Nineteen, Twenty, my plate's empty!

## BYE, BABY BUNTING

Bye, Bye Baby Bunting,
Daddy's gone a-hunting,
He's gone to get a rabbit skin
To wrap the Baby Bunting in.

## I'M A LITTLE TEAPOT

I'm a little teapot,
Short and stout.
Here is my handle,
Here is my spout.
When I get all steamed up,
Hear me shout!
Just tip me over,
And pour me out!

I'm a clever teapot,
Yes it's true.
I'll show you,
What I can do.
I can change my handle,
And my spout!
Just tip me over,
And pour me out!

Every parent and teacher of young children needs resources to help them remember oral traditions, especially poems and songs. These make wonderful gifts for birthdays, graduations, and holidays.

*Wee Sing Mother Goose* by Pamela Conn Beall (2006) is an hour of sing-alongs and finger plays. Parents and teachers can join in as they develop children's imaginations. The *Mother Goose Songbook* (1988) by Carol Barratt includes piano and guitar arrangements for twenty-eight nursery rhymes. Jaqueline Sinclair's playful pictures enhance this collection.

Nursery rhymes lend themselves to gestures like waving bye-bye and lifting up arms. Babies usually love to join in, using similar gestures. Be aware, however, that some babies are overly sensitive to touch.

Most babies outgrow this sensitivity, but a few need physical therapy to be comfortable with tickles and hugs. The rhythm of songs and poems are usually pleasant for young children, and also promote language development.

Mother Goose nursery rhymes have been handed down for centuries, even before they were written. They are in the public domain and are not protected by copyright laws.

In addition to hearing songs and nursery rhymes, babies and toddlers enjoy looking at Board Books read to them by their caregivers. Board books are usually illustrated with clear drawings or photos of everyday objects, such as cups and saucers, forks and spoons, and animals like birds, bugs, cats, dogs, fish and snakes. Insights K on page 38 offers a list of thirty-five board books.

The recent increase in the number of board books is very impressive, because their production requires more natural resources than other book formats. Modern board books, which are often made of cardboard or plastic, have stiff covers and pages that stand up to the chewing and drooling of teething babies.

Young children love to hold board books in their hands, but they have frequent food and drink spills, so most board books are made to be cleaned with mild soap and water. Cloth books can be tossed into a clothes washer or into a dishwasher.

Animals top the list of children's preferred topics, so backyard creatures like rabbits, snails, squirrels and turtles often inhabit board books. Other creatures, including working animals like dogs and horses, wild animals like antelope, and zoo animals like giraffes and zebras, are also typical subjects of board books.

The colorful and simple illustrations in board books are usually inviting, but rarely realistic. Until children are six years old, the beauty and clarity of illustrations are more important than realism.

Realism first becomes critical when young children begin to value books for factual information. Then board books should be replaced by standard 32-page Picture Books. Insights Q on page 68 presents fifty picture books.

Meanwhile, a well-designed physical environment for babies, toddlers and their caregivers, will support concept, language, and relationship development. In an appropriate learning environment, board books can be read over and over.

Furniture for babies and toddlers should include comfortable adult chairs for reading and rocking, as well as a sofa where caregivers can read to more than one child at a time. Listening to books is a long tradition that most children will come to love.

Insights K presents thirty-five good board books that children will enjoy. These can be borrowed from the library or purchased as gifts to be appreciated for years. The list below is organized alphabetically by authors' last names.

## Insights K: Thirty-Five Board Books For Children

*Peek-A-Boo Board Book* (1997) by Janet and Allan Ahlberg
*Baby Signs* (2008) by Joy Allen
*Please, Mr. Panda: A Board Book* (2016) by Steve Antony
*Bunnies!!! Board Book* (2018) by Kevan Atteberry (Illustrator)
*Little Green* (2005) by Keith Baker, A Red Wagon Book
*Boats Board Book* (1998) by Byron Barton
*The Water Hole, A Counting Book* (2001) by Graeme Base
*The Twelve Days of Christmas* (2004) by Jan Brett

*Clifford Counts 1, 2, 3* (1998) by Norman Bridwell
*My World* (2003) by Margaret Wise Brown and Clement Hurd
*Little Cloud* (1998) by Eric Carle
*Have You Seen My Cat?* (2009) Slide and Peek Book by Eric Carle
*Bugs at Work* (1997) Busy Bugs Board Books by David A. Carter
*Fruits in Suits* (2017) by Jared Chapman
*First 100 Farm Words* (2010) by Sarah Creese
*Little Polar Bear* (1999) by Hans de Beer
*The Pout-Pout Fish* (2018) by Deborah Diesen
*Peas on Earth* (2012) by Todd H. Doodler
*Baby Animals* (2008) by Gyo Fujikawa
*Sheila Rae's Peppermint Stick* (2001) by Kevin Henkes
*Spot's First Christmas* (2003) by Eric Hill and Margaret Frith
*Construction Zone* (1999) by Tana Hoban
*Play Baby Play!* (2012) by Marilyn Janovitz
*Rock-A-Bye Baby* (2011) by John Kanzler, Effie I. Canning
*Leo the Late Bloomer* (1998) by Robert Kraus and José Aruego
*The Carrot Seed* (1993) by Ruth Krauss and Crocket Johnson
*The Owl and the Pussycat* (1997) by Edward Lear and Jan Brett
*Five Little Pumpkins* (2010) by Ben Mantle (Illustrator)
*Pooh and Some Bees* (1996) by A. A. Milne and Ernest H. Shepard
*The Night Before Christmas* (1991) by Clement Clarke Moore
*The Icky Bug Alphabet Book* (2000) by Jerry Pallotta and Ralph Masiello
*Ladybug Girl and Her Papa* (2017) by Dave Soman, Jacky Davis
*Old MacDonald* (1998) by Rosemary Wells
*Shoes Board Book* (1995) by Elizabeth Winthrop, William Joyce
*Silly Sally* (2007) by Audrey Wood

# CHAPTER 3

# Communication for Toddlers: 1 to 3 Years

Toddlers are very observant as they learn about their surroundings. My one-year-old granddaughter notices every speck of lint on the carpet. Then she puts it into her mouth for further examination.

Toddlers are especially tuned in to experiences with body language, books read aloud, environmental print, expressive art and music, pretend play, rhythm and poetry, and self-agency.

Toddlers notice much more than an adult's tone of voice. With toddlers, adults need to watch their body language. Shouting across a room should be saved for emergency situations when adults must catch a child's attention.

> "Don't throw that block, Amy! You could hurt someone."
> "Everybody freeze! I think I hear the fire alarm."
> "Drop those scissors, Tom! They're dangerous."
> "Stop! Please wait by the door till I get there."

Adults need to be physically close to toddlers when talking to them. They should be face-to-face on the toddler's level, and try to make eye contact. Grown-ups will touch toddlers in an inviting way, using pats and hugs, holding hands, and often offering a lap for snuggles.

If adults are fun but gentle in their approach, toddlers will want to stay close by. Pleasant adults will be imitated. These grown-ups will become the toddlers' models for language development.

Infants seem to communicate with their whole bodies, whether they're wriggling with pleasure or thrashing around with frustration. But when toddlers are about twelve to eighteen months, they begin to use eye movements, hand signals, and spoken words to communicate.

My year-old granddaughter had typically limited language skills, but she could ask for her favorite song by signing *apple* or *banana*.

### A SONG ABOUT FRUIT
by Theresa M. Sull

Oh, give me some fruit,
I don't give a hoot,
But my very favorite fruit,
Is banana!
An orange is okay,
Or an apple a day,
But my favorite,
Absolutely
Is banana!

Research demonstrates that when caregivers provide more language stimulation and more involved care, children will perform better in elementary school on measures of thinking and language. Understanding basic concepts of child development will help adults meet the challenges of interacting with toddlers.

Toddlers are in a terrific but demanding stage, the recognition of their autonomy. In *Toddlers and Parents: A Declaration of Independence* (1989), Dr. T. Berry Brazelton describes toddlers' age-appropriate struggle for individuality.

In *The Magic Years: Understanding and Handling the Problems of Early Childhood* (1996), Selma H. Fraiberg uses anecdotes to illuminate the sometimes baffling behavior of toddlers.

*No Bad Kids: Toddler Discipline Without Shame* was published in 2014 by Janet Lansbury. Her advice was based on education and twenty years of working with families. Lansbury was a student of Magda Gerber, an early childhood educator who taught parents and other teachers to understand babies and treat them with respect.

Toddlers come to realize that they are separate from their caregivers. They are people with unique ideas and desires, which is why toddlers discover the power of the word NO. They also learn to express themselves with grunts, squeals, and other strong sounds, including banging on pots, or pounding on piano keys.

Dancing is another form of self-expression for toddlers. Although their moves might look like jumping or wiggling, toddlers are really responding to the rhythm of the music.

To support this dancing, adults can collect simple instruments like tambourines and tom-toms. Shakers can be made from empty plastic containers filled with dried rice or beans. Large pots become drums when they are beaten with wooden spoons.

Banging on household objects might sound like noise to adults, but this form of self-expression leads to later expressive abilities like speaking and writing. Children's response to the rhythm of music is related to their later response to the rhythms of language.

Toddlers are developing the initiative necessary for maturation, but their creative actions can cause problems for others. That's why toddlers, more than older children, are sometimes abused. Adults easily can manage toddlers with their much bigger bodies.

Grown-ups should never pull a toddler's arm with a jerk, or lift a toddler by one arm. These common actions could require a trip to a hospital emergency room to mend a preventable injury.

The large knobs at the end of a toddler's bones can slip out of their sockets because these bones are not fully developed. A toddler's arm can be dislocated more easily than an adult's, possibly causing a stretched ligament.

My husband was embarrassed when our daughter injured herself walking on a low shelf in a department store. His six-foot height had caused the problem. Her father was holding Linnet by one hand when she slipped off the shelf, jerking her arm out of its socket at the elbow.

Linnet also went to the emergency room when her father and a babysitter playfully swung Linnet by her hands and feet. Because that ligament had been stretched before, her arm bone popped out of its socket again.

The doctor asked her father questions to eliminate child abuse. Embarrassed, Gene learned a lesson. Small children enjoy and need rough and tumble play, but adults must monitor themselves to protect children's smaller bodies.

Pulling a toddler by the arm seems especially shortsighted if the goal is to raise a writer. Toddlers should associate pleasure, not pain, with their fingers, wrists, elbows and shoulders.

Our second daughter Julia never needed a trip to the hospital for an accident. We'd learned that every child needs gentle, caring touches. Body language will say so much!

Reasoning with a child will promote language development, including the ability to listen. Adults always speak softly to a toddler who's being appropriately childish.

Grown-ups must never act out in anger because they could accidentally and easily injure a child.

When speaking to toddlers, adults must match their body language to their words. For example, grown-ups should look serious if they really are serious, and look proud if they're proud.

While toddlers are learning language at such a remarkable rate, they use all the available clues to understand spoken words. Adults' gestures can improve children's language development, quickly increasing communication competence.

To indicate approval of a toddler's actions, grown-ups should try to nod and smile a lot. They can raise their eyebrows to show interest or open their hands to indicate awe at what they hear or see. They can cup their ears if they want a child to speak louder, or put a finger to their lips if they want the child to be quieter.

When grown-ups use body language to clarify their words, they're increasing children's receptive language skills. To encourage a toddler's growing expressive language skills, Reflective Listening is the best tool to use.

Reflective Listening refers to the action of listening to and looking at a child very carefully. Then the adult states what they've understood about what's happening. Sometimes the ongoing situation provides enough clues to clarify the child's meaning.

Reflective Listening can make a child's intentions evident. Then an older person can model oral language at the exact time that children are motivated to learn about specific grammar and words.

Educational research shows that gentle modeling of the correct grammar is more effective than pointing out children's mistakes.

Child: Cookie! Cookie!
Adult: You're hungry for cookies. Can I have a cookie too?

Child: Hate you!
Adult: You're angry with me now. You don't want to stop playing.

Child: Gots mouses.
Adult: I like this picture of mice, too. Let's count the mice.

As toddlers tune in to language, and the adults around them use Reflective Listening, the toddlers' Expressive Language takes off.

Psychologists and speech pathologists can record and transcribe children's spontaneous words to assess their progress with language. Specialists also can identify the parts of speech that children use, such as nouns, verbs, adjectives, adverbs, conjunctions, prepositions, pronouns and interjections.

Professionals can determine a child's average number of words that are used in one phrase or sentence. This is called the Mean Length of Utterance, or MLU. By determining MLU, experts can learn whether a child's language is progressing well, or whether some language intervention is required.

For the first few years, MLU corresponds roughly to the child's age. A one-year-old child usually utters one word at a time, and at two years uses two-word phrases. When a child is four, some phrases or sentences are longer than four words, but MLU is often 4.0 when an average length is computed.

It's not always easy to identify one utterance. Toddlers use pointing and grunting to express themselves, as well as recognizable words. Additionally, they often repeat themselves, which makes identifying one utterance even more difficult.

Insights L consists of recorded language samples. Linnet was always active, so she was recorded during the few moments she was calmly eating, playing with toys, or watching television. Then her utterances were laboriously transcribed.

Linnet's Expressive Language became much more complex in only a few months.

## Insights L: Toddler Language Sample

LINNET AT 19 MONTHS

I do it, Daddy
Go away Mommy
Help
Deedle, deedle, deedle (*Linnet's word for tickle*)
Bye Mommy pooh (*when a toilet flushes*)
He talking
Talking here (*Does Linnet mean* hear?)
That
Yeah
There
Baby, baby, baby, baby, baby, baby
Yep
Mummy, mummy, mummy, mummy
What is that, Mommy? (*When she hears the sink drain*)
Baby, baby, baby, baby, baby
See Daddy, See Daddy
I talkin, I talkin, I talkin, I talkin, I talkin
Hot piz (*pizza*)
All gone Daddy (*His pizza is finished*)

## LINNET AT 24 MONTHS

Mommy, help me
Help me make baby crib
Um, right there
I got it here
I wanna color my own
My crayons
Clean eh up gether
I clean baby's crib up
Yeah, together
Daddy's bringin me my block
Thank you, Daddy, thank you
There. What you doing?
Not your blocks, my blocks
Baby bring your blocks?
Lady (referring to the movie, *Lady and the Tramp*)
Thank you Lady, Thank you Lady
Bringin my blocks
Look, Hi!
Yeah, she do it all work
What baby doin?
Kicking, kicking

As toddlers begin to talk, grown-ups should encourage all their efforts. Adults can use enjoyable language by repeating nursery rhymes, such as those in Insights J on page 31. Soon the adults will begin to read aloud longer poems.

When Julia was four, she reversed our roles by teaching me a poem she'd learned at preschool. I found *One Misty, Moisty Morning* in *Childcraft: Poems of Early Childhood* (1939). Grown-ups can teach toddlers rhymes they remember from their own childhoods.

# ONE MISTY, MOISTY MORNING
(Anonymous Mother Goose Rhyme)

One misty, moisty morning,
When cloudy was the weather,
I chanced to meet an old man
Clothed all in leather:
He began to compliment,
And I began to grin—
"How do you do?"
And "How do you do?"
And "How do you do?" again!

Robert Lewis Stevenson was born in 1850 in Edinburgh, Scotland. The novelist and poet is known for works like *Treasure Island*, *Kidnapped*, and *A Child's Garden of Verses*. Published in 1885, Stevenson's collection of children's poetry is a classic. In 2018, Createspace printed a new edition.

# THE SWING
by Robert Louis Stevenson

How do you like to go up in a swing,
Up in the air so blue?
Oh, I do think it the pleasantest thing
Ever a child can do!

Up in the air and over the wall,
Till I can see so wide,
Rivers and trees and cattle and all
Over the countryside —

Till I look down on the garden green,
Down on the roof so brown —
Up in the air I go flying again,
Up in the air and down!

*Polish* was the language I heard at the priests' rec grandmother worked as a housekeeper. Although I spent a vacations staying with my grandmother, I never learned to read or Polish beyond a few polite words and phrases, and a Polish nurse rhyme my mother chanted.

My daughter Julia, however, chose Polish to fulfill her foreign language requirement in college. Because few American students try to learn a difficult Eastern European language, the Polish classes were very small and included some native Polish speakers.

The students enjoyed lots of attention from their teacher, and they often interacted among themselves. So Julia picked up a lot of Polish, including several songs in that language. My mother, who was raised speaking Polish, still enjoys singing with Julia.

Feelings of belongingness made the Polish classes enjoyable, and also increased students' motivation for learning. Just as several educational researchers had demonstrated, learning will improve when students experience relatedness.

Families need a book of children's poetry to dip into every day. Inexpensive poetry books are easy to find in bookstores or on-line.

A *Treasury of Children's Poetry* (1998), edited by Alison Sage, contains rhymes for the very young, as well as more challenging poetry by writers like William Blake and William Shakespeare.

### MICE
by Rose Fyleman

I think mice
Are rather nice.
Their tails are long,
Their faces small,

ey haven't any
Chins at all.
eir ears are pink,
eir teeth are white,
They run about
The house at night.
They nibble things
They shouldn't touch
And no one seems
To like them much.
But I think mice
Are nice.

### MITTEN SONG
by Mary Louise Allen

"Thumbs in the thumb place,
Fingers all together!"
This is the song
We sing in mitten weather,
When it is cold,
It doesn't matter whether
Mittens are wool,
Or made of finest leather.
This is the song
We sing in mitten weather:
"Thumbs in the thumb place,
Fingers all together!"

If parents and other teachers read poetry to children when they are
very young, soon the children will begin to compose their own poems.
At first, children's poetry will imitate the meanings, rhythm, and
vocabulary of the poems that they heard.

Proud parents will send copies of children's poem relatives.

A few children might have compositions published commercially my daughter Julia, but even if children never write for publication, they'll need to write well to be successful in school. Wise adults read poetry and stories to older children, too.

Just think about these numbers for a minute. If you read only one book aloud at bedtime, starting before your child's first birthday until she's five years old, you will have read about 1,450 children's books to her before she enters kindergarten. This huge number includes favorite books read over and over, because repetition is necessary to consolidate learning.

Because children's books are so short, why not read two books every evening? If you do that, your child will have heard almost 3,000 stories read aloud before kindergarten!

Toddlers love to hear and to look at books, enjoying any new information about their world. Caregivers will keep a few appropriate books handy to take advantage of teachable moments.

Toddlers learn a lot by touching, so don't let them loose in a bookstore or library where they might damage books that don't belong to them. Strollers can be helpful, even after children can walk by themselves.

## Insights M: Twelve Tips On Reading Aloud

1. Hold a baby or toddler on your lap; Preschoolers sit beside you.

2. Hold the book so that children can easily view the cover.

3. Announce the title of the book while pointing to it.

nor and Illustrator; Say that authors write
draw and paint the pictures.

I clearly, with an animated expression.

ces for characters that sound funny, sad, scary...

ter each page, make comments on the action or illustration.

8. Don't be preachy or *teachy* but indicate wonder and interest.

9. Let a child turn the page when you say, *"Ready, turn!"*

10. Ask questions (*Which cat do you like? Where's the dog?*)

11. For older preschoolers, ask questions that require reasoning:
    (*How will they do that? Why do they want that?*)

12. Make connections between books and real life.
    (*That looks like our cabinet; We have a cat, too!*)

Over hundreds of years, books written especially for children have become standardized. Originally, the individual printer decided on the number of pages in a children's book.

Eventually, all printers settled on the presently standard 32 pages, including end papers, title page and author's biography. Eight pages can fold smoothly into a SIGNATURE. More pages would be too thick to fold and bind easily.

Because 32 is divisible by 4, books of 32 pages result in less wasted paper, which makes a book less costly. The author traditionally chose the topics and composed the text that would comfort, educate, frighten, interest, or reassure a typical child.

Modern children's authors have broad knowledge of child development and familiarity with characters' environments, whether rural, suburban or urban.

Children's stories rarely contain details associated with differing eras or locations. Such anachronisms will jar audiences by interfering with their "willing suspension of disbelief." This phrase, introduced by Samuel Taylor Coleridge in 1817, refers to the ability of an audience to temporarily accept fiction as reality.

Earlier authors and playwrights like William Shakespeare had already noted that audience satisfaction required pretense on the part of both actors and audiences.

Anachronisms, therefore, can be used intentionally to interject meaning through contrast. Only a very talented writer like Mark Twain, who wrote *A Connecticut Yankee in King Arthur's Court* (1889) or Lynn Reid Banks, author of *The Indian in the Cupboard* (1980), can manage this with grace.

Parents and other teachers can encourage singing and movement in toddlers with carefully selected CDs, DVDs, and TV programs. Although some people ridiculed the slow pace of Fred McFeely Rogers, his program exactly matched the educational needs of my daughters. They both loved *Mr. Rogers' Neighborhood.*

*Sesame Street*, another long-running television program, also supported learning and literacy. Three-year-old Julia read her first word independently when she was watching *Sesame Street*. "Car!" she said in surprise, "I read that word!"

Children benefit from watching positive TV programs that are not scary or violent. Other educational television programs are found on Public Television (PBS) and at *www.pbskids.org.*

At eighteen months, toddlers begin to express themselves through pre-drawing and pre-writing activities. One activity young children enjoy is scribbling over the pages of a coloring book, with no attempt to color within the lines.

Don't stop them! They're already responding to art, scribbling in a purposeful way, relating to the artist's marks on the page. Visual art appeals to many toddlers. When children are young, wise adults encourage toddlers' scribbles, getting their early drawing and writing skills off to a strong start.

Toddlers are able to hold crayons, pencils, non-toxic markers, and thick pieces of chalk in their fists. When she was only two, my granddaughter Abby purposefully scribbled notes to communicate with me. I treasured every delightful page.

Toddlers also enjoy finger painting with instant pudding or ketchup. They'll play with squirts of ketchup and mustard, intrigued by blending colors yellow and red to make orange.

Toddlers usually smear their faces, hair and clothing, so adults won't use real paint or liquid soap for finger painting. Toddlers are likely to taste these substances or poke them into their eyes.

Preschool and school-age children learn that hands must be kept away from eyes and mouth when painting. At first, occasionally smearing around an edible substance like ketchup, mustard, or pudding will provide tactile stimulation for children. Adults can draw alphabet letters, faces or numerals in this edible paint.

Young children enjoy these unusual art experiences, but it's too early to teach toddlers to draw or to write. Early childhood specialists confirm that sooner is not always better. Just appreciate the fun toddlers have with a variety of malleable substances.

Keep all writing tools out of a toddler's reach until an older person is able to supervise their use, or you could find unwanted marks on your walls. I painstakingly spent hours erasing my daughter's pencil lines from the wallpaper in a rented apartment.

Soon you'll be able to date and save children's drawings in a portfolio, or send scribbles and drawings to appreciative aunts, friends and grandparents. If a child talks about their scribbles, you can write a caption on them. Or you can simply write *a drawing by Timmy, age 20 months.*

A powerful message is sent when adults consider children's artwork worth saving and displaying.

Adults will have places to display children's artwork at home and in preschools. High bulletin boards out of children's reach are best.

Parents can tape children's drawings to mirrors, or can use magnets on refrigerators and file cabinets. Baseboard molding works well to support long sheets of Plexiglas®, creating a clear plastic display frame. Behind this frame children's drawings will be protected.

When adults display children's artwork and talk about it, toddlers will begin to think, "I am an artist." This early affirmation helps children take the risks necessary for learning in elementary school and beyond, when communication competence will be crucial to academic success.

Russian psychologist Lev Vygotsky emphasized the critical role of adults in children's development. Knowledgeable caregivers will scaffold a child's learning, offering the right support at exactly the right time.

Just as scaffolding on a construction site helps workers reach a spot at a specific time, scaffolding is impermanent and will be shifted as required.

Play provides a scaffold for children to support representation.

By engaging in pretend play with toddlers, adults are teaching the children that they can represent the real world through imagination. When we pretend to drink out of a toy cup, we are not really taking in liquid, but we still say to the child, "Yum! What delicious tea!"

Representation is practiced using toys. Healthy toddlers become emotionally attached to certain of their toys, such as building blocks, dolls, or stuffed animals like teddy bears. Children will use these toys to represent events in their own lives, the true beginning of creative composition.

My brother Michael had a favorite toy bulldog he called Winston. Winston seemed to be a more masculine toy than a doll, but could be loved and played with in the same way. As a toddler, my daughter Linnet would put her baby doll to bed under a towel on the kitchen floor, imitating the way I tucked her into bed at night.

Examples in museums prove that toys have been used by children for over 3000 years! Pretend play has been encouraging human creativity for a very long time.

Providing safe toys for toddlers is one way to scaffold pretend play. For older preschoolers, scaffolding may involve buying or building a playhouse or a puppet theater.

Understanding representation, a concept developed through pretend play, will be critical to thinkers in the future. When students start to learn a second language, for example, they begin by letting a new word represent an old concept. The French words *le chien* will stand for the concept of *a dog*.

Mathematicians often use one symbol to represent another in an algebraic equation. Each side of an equation contains one or more terms. The most famous equation was written by Albert Einstein.

$E = mc^2$ stated that the energy of a physical system is equal to the product of its mass and the speed of light squared.

Without the basic concept of representation, human beings would not have the innumerable benefits of scientific progress. There would be no automatic transmissions and no computers.

The famous American writer Tennessee Williams practiced representation playing with his sister. He let broken bits of glass from the trash stand for diamonds, emeralds, rubies and sapphires.

Adults who write novels or screenplays are still pretending and getting paid for that pretense. That's why knowledgable parents and other teachers encourage children's play. Play really can lead to treasure!

When their children are toddlers, parents and teachers can begin to point out environmental print, such as the STOP sign on the corner, or the street signs on their neighborhood walks. When environmental print becomes a focus, children will begin to recognize these familiar signs, and soon begin to create their own.

The adults in their lives also can create personal environmental print for children. They can label objects in the house or childcare center with simple hand-lettered signs, such as *chair, chest, clock, desk, door, hamper, microwave, piano, refrigerator, sink, sofa, stove, table, television* or *window.*

# CHAPTER 4
# Reading Aloud to Foster Communication

In *One Writer's Beginnings*, author Eudora Welty remembered, "I learned from the age of two or three that any room in our house, at any time of day, was there to be read in, or to be read to."

Thomas Jefferson had an extensive library, the largest collection of books owned by one person in the United States. In 1814 the British burned the Library of Congress. Jefferson offered to sell his library of almost 10,000 volumes to Congress to replace books demolished by the British, and would accept any price. Congress bought 6,500 books from Jefferson, doubling the number lost.

Abraham Lincoln was a noted orator even before he became president. As a boy, Abraham Lincoln read his schoolbooks propped in front of the fireplace. As a man, his Emancipation Proclamation changed the lives of more Americans than any other speech. Yet its somewhat bland language, compared to the eloquence of the Gettysburg Address, was dismissed as unworthy.

In 2004, author Allen C. Guelzo published *Lincoln's Emancipation Proclamation: The End of Slavery in America*. Guelzo dispels mistakes and myths around the Emancipation Proclamation and explains how Abraham Lincoln wrote the world's greatest declaration of freedom.

Helen Keller (1880-1968) was a prolific author and a political activist. She was the first deaf-blind person to earn a bachelor's degree. Her teacher Anne Sullivan taught Keller to read and write by spelling words into the palm of her hand. Helen Keller's birthplace in Tuscumbia, Alabama is presently a museum.

Keller was well-traveled and outspoken as a lecturer. She campaigned for women's right to vote, labor rights, socialism and similar causes. Helen Keller wrote a total of 12 published books, including *The Story of My Life, Optimism, The World I Live In, The Open Door, Out of the Dark,* and *Peace at Eventide.*

## Insights N: Ten Ways To Provide Book Experiences

1. Rotate children's books that are accessible much of the day.

2. Read books over and over, until children supply missing words.

3. Read children a variety of books, including alphabet books biographies, counting books, fables, fairy tales, fantasy, history, humor, nursery rhymes, poetry books, real-life accounts, science books, sports books, and books on wildlife.

4. Read books to inspire dance, art, or cooking projects.

5. Give children hardback books to slowly fill their shelves.

6. Make homemade books with children.

7. Take children on field trips to bookstores, libraries, or schools.

8. Take children's dictation as they explain their artwork.

9. Read back what you write, so children hear their own words

10. Invite children to illustrate their stories as gifts to families.

Children need a multitude of experiences with books. The more they hear books, the more that they will want to hear books. Children are comforted by repetition because people possess an internal body clock. They are active, hungry, sleepy or wakeful at about the same time each day, so they appreciate daily routines.

The routine called Listening Time, Story Time, Book Time, or Time-to-Read can be introduced with a poem or a song, like those in Insights O, below.

Adults could create a dreamy tune for the STORY TIME SONG and a melody for READING AND LISTENING TIME.

The intriguing poem TO START STORY TIME is a challenging invitation for older children.

When they have enjoyable memories of listening to books, soon the children will remind their caregivers about Reading Time.

## Insights O: How To Introduce Reading Time

### STORY TIME SONG

Time to draw near; What shall we hear?
I'd like to READ to you now.
Please choose a seat; And let me repeat,
I'd LOVE to read to you now!

### READING AND LISTENING TIME

It's reading time and listening time,
I'm going to share a book.
Attention, please, it's lots of fun,
These pictures need a look!

## TO START STORY TIME

When you open a book,
Certain things might fly out,
Things that can beckon,
And things that can shout.
When you open a book,
You could even be caught,
By a thing that you may not
Have known that you sought!

Knowledgeable parents and other teachers read books to children for at least ten educational reasons.

## Insights P: Ten Reasons To Read Books Aloud

1. To entertain children

2. To enhance language development

3. To promote literacy

4. As bibliotherapy

5. To teach values

6. To enrich multicultural understanding

7. To increase knowledge

8. To inspire creativity

9. As a management tool

10. To engage children in lifelong learning

The First reason to read aloud is to entertain children. Good books are entertaining, whether the stories inspire laughter or tears. Children will sit spellbound listening to a well-written story or poem, and often ask for their favorites again.

Go ahead! Read a favorite over and over. When children ask for repetition, they want to enjoy that pleasurable feeling again. Repetition also strengthens children's learning. The language that young children hear contributes to their speaking, reading, and writing skills when they're older.

Word Play (or wordplay) is a literary technique in which specific words are used to produce an intended effect, often mainly for fun. Word Play includes alliteration, consonance, double meanings, puns, rhymes and rhythm.

*The Piggy in the Puddle* (1974), written by Charlotte Pomerantz and illustrated by James Marshall, is a book that will tickle children with its tongue-twisting Word Play. Dr. Seuss proved an earlier master of Word Play in *Green Eggs and Ham* (1960). In 2007, Emily Gravett published *Orange Pear Apple Bear*. In 2010, *Word Play: Rhyming Grades K-1* was produced by Carson-Dellosa.

The Second reason to read books out loud is to enhance children's language development. The context of a story provides clues to the meaning and use of new vocabulary, and demonstrates various grammatical structures, or the order of words in phrases and sentences. English word order is commonly Subject, Verb, Object.

A number of classic children's books originally written in English, can now be found in French, German, Russian, Spanish, and other languages. At an age when young children are biologically primed for language learning, they will enjoy comparing written words in more than one language.

For over 75 years, Dover Publications has provided inexpensive books for adults and children at *doverpublications.com*. Here you can find excellent, illustrated dual language books by Hayward Cirker and Barbara Steadman.

Their collection offers basic words in several languages, including English, French, German, Hebrew, Italian, Japanese and Spanish.

Ruth Heller is an English language vocabulary builder in books like *A Cache of Jewels and Other Collective Nouns* (1981), and *Animals Born Alive and Well: A Book About Mammals* (1999).

In *The Year at Maple Hill Farm* (1978), Alice and Martin Provensen demonstrate grammar and provide information about animals, people and plants living in rural areas. A variety of similes are found in *Quick as a Cricket* (1994), written by Audrey Wood and illustrated by Don Wood. Alliteration is language enhancement in *Slowly, Slowly, Slowly, Said the Sloth* (2002) by Eric Carle.

The Third reason to read books aloud is to promote literacy with pre-reading skills. Children's realization that marks on paper can represent spoken words is demonstrated by Jan Pienkowski. A pioneer of pop-up books, Pienkowski pairs written names with pop-up pictures in *Dinner Time, Little Monsters,* and *Pizza!*

Two Insights offer more information about pre-reading skills. See *Seven Basic Concepts of Literacy* on page six, and *Physical & Communication Development* on page eighteen.

The Fourth reason to read aloud is for bibliotherapy, or using realistic stories to solve emotional problems. Kids will be relieved that they share common experiences with storybook characters.

Then they'll be reassured when the characters in books find solutions to their problems.

A variety of books evoke this empathy. In *Look at Me* (1979), written by Charlotte Hall Ricks and illustrated by Annie Gusman, Catherine can't get her busy mother's attention, although she really tries. *Will I Have a Friend?* (1989) by Miriam Cohen, is illustrated by Lillian Hoban. In this book, a boy worries he won't make a new friend when he enters school.

Another heroine thinks of escaping, in *A Baby Sister for Frances,* written by Russell Hoban (2011). Lillian Hoban is again the talented illustrator.

The Fifth reason for reading to children also involves identification with the characters in books. As children vicariously experience life in books, they actually learn about real-life values. They develop morals that they'll use when faced with situations previously encountered by favorite characters in stories.

In quality books for children, heavy topics are treated with a light touch. *Nana Upstairs and Nana Downstairs* (1997) by Tomie dePaola, explores old age and death. These topics are examined in a different context in *The Tenth Good Thing About Barney* (1987) by Judith Viorst, when a family pet dies. Gary Kurz wrote *Wagging Tails In Heaven: The Gift of Our Pets' Everlasting Love,* in 2011.

The Sixth reason to read aloud is for multicultural understanding. Whatever their ethnic backgrounds, children could feel empathy with the characters in a book.

Through a variety of good reads, children easily can enter our increasingly diverse society. Given the proliferation of travel and worldwide connections made possible through email, telephone, and websites, today's children will become citizens of the globe.

In *Everybody Cooks Rice* (1995), written by Norah Dooley with pictures by Peter J. Thornton, children discover that neighbors from Barbados, China, Haiti, India, Northern Italy, Puerto Rico and Vietnam all have rice for dinner.

In *Cleversticks* (1995), written by Bernard Ashley and illustrated by Derek Brazell, Ling Sung discovers that his skill with chopsticks impresses the class.

Emery Bernhard tells how babies are carried world-wide in *A Ride on Mother's Back: A Day of Baby Carrying Around the World* (1996), with illustrations by Durga Bernhard. Ezra Jack Keats illustrates stories like *The Snowy Day* (2007) with African-American children. In 2007, Vera B. Williams shows a slice of city life in *A Chair for My Mother*.

The Seventh reason to read aloud is so books can increase general knowledge. This will set children off on the correct academic foot.

My daughters liked *Auto Mechanic* (*Work People Do*), written in 1989 by Betsy Imershein, so they could understand their father's workday. *Going to Day Care* by Fred Rogers (1985) provides a glimpse of kids' and teachers' typical days in a childcare center. In *Carl Goes to Daycare* by Alexandra Day (1993), Carl the Rottweiler takes charge at the childcare center where he's visiting.

When a story's action takes place in an unfamiliar country or in times past, books can introduce different animals and plants to children, and can describe uncommon cultures.

Children will enjoy *Caps for Sale: A Tale of a Peddler, Some Monkeys and Their Monkey Business,* written and illustrated by Esphyr Slobodkina in 1999. In a sequel, *More Caps for Sale: Another Tale of Mischievous Monkeys,* Ann Marie Mulhearn Sayer aided Slobodkina in 2015.

In a 1993 fantasy, *Ming Lo Moves the Mountain* by Arnold Lobel, Ming Lo's wife asks him to move a bothersome mountain. To start a new series, the best-selling author Neil Patrick Harris published *The Magic Misfits* in 2017.

So that children can comprehend the clever actions of these characters, such complicated books bear re-reading. Other books clarify concepts like number, sequence, shape, size and time, in stories that have fascinated children for generations.

In 1928, Wanda Gág wrote and illustrated *Millions of Cats*. Her masterpiece is the oldest picture book in print in the United States. Now more than ninety years old, the book continues to bewitch and to enchant new listeners.

*The Carrot Seed* (1945) by Ruth Krauss, with pictures by Crockett Johnson, has never been out of print. The story of the faith and patience needed to grow things is triumphant.

What happens when a family of ducks visits a swimming pool? *The Number 10 Duckling* (1972), written by Betty Rosendall and illustrated by Tom Dunnington, is a counting book. Children can practice *Counting Wildflowers* (1986) in Bruce Degen's book.

*The Ugly Duckling* by Hans Christian Anderson (1995) is a classic about early awkwardness. *Way to Go: Finding Your Way with a Compass* by Sharon Smith (2000) provides tools to explore nature. *Discover the World of Bugs* by Peraboni and Banfi (2018) brings nature study up-to-date.

The Eighth reason to read aloud is for books to inspire children's creativity. Teachers and parents can use drama, drawing, movement, painting, rhythm and song to increase creativity.

*Jamberry* (2008) by Bruce Degen inspires artistic responses with jazzy text and dreamy illustrations. Creative thinking is inspired by *A House Is a House for Me* (2007), cleverly written by Mary Ann Hoberman with pictures by Betty Fraser. In 2017, Jo Witek wrote *In My Room: A Book of Creativity and Imagination,* where a little girl can be anyone and go anywhere.

The Ninth reason to read to children is that listening to books can be a management tool. Controlling children's excitement, aiding in transitions, and managing children's movements at home or in school are very useful tools.

"Let's listen to a story," a caregiver could say to calm the children, easing the transitions to hand washing and table setting before lunch. Favorite books can quiet children before chores.

*Goodnight Moon* (2011) and *The Runaway Bunny* (2017), both written by Margaret Wise Brown with pictures by Clement Hurd, are creatively calming during transitions. These books can be enjoyed again and again.

But caution is required. Reading should be used for enjoyment and learning, but rarely to control children's movements. To smooth transitions, however, an engaging book can't be beat!

The Tenth and most important reason for reading aloud is to engage children in the habit of lifelong learning. Even in today's highly computerized world, where searches on the Internet can yield an overwhelming amount of information, knowledge is most accessible in books.

Books provide more information than magazines, movies, or television programs. The details in books can educate readers about current events, historical facts and supposition, and conjecture about the future.

A book can be read anywhere: in bed, on the beach, on a bus, in a doctor's waiting room, at the kitchen table, lounging around the swimming pool, in a restaurant or on the sofa. So many worthwhile books have been written that people will never exhaust the number of great books they can read in the future.

Insights Q lists fifty picture books to read aloud to young children. These books are listed alphabetically by the author's last name.

## Insights Q: Fifty Picture Books To Read Aloud

*A Special Day for Mommy* (2004) by Dan Andreasen
*Grandfather Buffalo* (2006) by Jim Arnosky
*Happy Birthday, Moon* (1982) by Frank Asch
*Monsieur Saguette and His Baguette* (2004) by Frank Asch
*The Skunk: A Picture Book* (2015) by Mac Barnett
*A Ride on Mother's Back* (1996) by Emery Bernhard
*December* (1997) by Eve Bunting
*The Very Hungry Caterpillar* (1969) by Eric Carle
*The Magic Rabbit* (2013) by Annette LeBlanc Cate
*Will I Have a Friend?* (1967) by Miriam Cohen
*Nana Upstairs and Nana Downstairs* (1973) by Tomie dePaola
*Jamberry* (1985) by Bruce Degen
*Everybody Cooks Rice* (1992) by Norah Dooley
*The Squirrel Manifesto* (2018) by Ric and Jean Edelman
*Jeanne-Marie Counts Her Sheep* (1951) by Francoise
*Corduroy* (1968) by Don Freeman
*Millions of Cats* (1928) by Wanda Gág
*The King Who Rained* (1970) by Fred Gwynne
*Bread and Jam for Frances* (1964) by Russell Hoban
*A House Is a House for Me* (1978) by Mary Ann Hoberman
*Moon Mouse* (1969) by Adelaide Holl
*Auto Mechanics (Work People Do)* (1989) by Betsy Imershein
*The Snowy Day* (1962) by Ezra Jack Keats
*Whose Mouse Are You?* (1970) by Robert Kraus
*The Carrot Seed* (1945) by Ruth Krauss
*Swimmy* (1967) by Leo Lionni
*Ming Lo Moves the Mountain* (1982) by Arnold Lobel
*There's a Nightmare in My Closet* (1968) by Mercer Mayer

*Tikki Tikki Tembo* (1968) by Arlene Mosel

*Mr. Monkey and the Gotcha Bird* (1984) by Walter Dean Myers

*Dinnertime* (1981) by Jan Pienkowski

*The Little Engine That Could* (1930) by Watty Piper

*The Piggy in the Puddle* (1974) by Charlotte Pomerantz

*The Tale of Peter Rabbit* (1902) by Beatrix Potter

*A Book of Seasons* (1976) by Alice and Martin Provensen

*Curious George* (1941) by H. A. Rey

*Pretzel* (1944) by Margret Rey

*Benje, The Squirrel Who Lost His Tail* (1969) by Elizabeth Rice

*Look at Me* (1979) by Charlotte Hall Ricks

*Tar Beach* (1991) by Faith Ringgold

*Going to Day Care* (1985) by Fred McFeely Rogers

*Rain Makes Applesauce* (1964) by Julian Scheer

*Where The Wild Things Are* (1963) by Maurice Sendak

*How The Grinch Stole Christmas* (1957) by Dr. Seuss

*Every Thing On It* (2011) by Shel Silverstein

*A Chair for My Mother* (1982) by Vera B. Williams

*Bear Snores On* (2002) by Karma Wilson

*Quick as a Cricket* (1982) by Audrey Wood

*Harry the Dirty Dog* (1956) by Gene Zion

*Mr. Rabbit and the Lovely Present* (1962) by Charlotte Zolotow

These picture books are truly entertaining for children. But don't stop with my suggestions! Use them as a starting point to gather a collection of your own favorites.

Take other suggestions from TV shows like *Reading Rainbow,* the most-watched PBS program in classrooms. Featuring over 150 episodes, *Reading Rainbow* hosted by Lavar Burton, aired for more than twenty years. The website *pbskids.org* introduces a *host* of great books.

Find free book lists at a public library. Order books on the websites *amazon.com* and *alibris.com.* Inexpensive books are found at *doverpublications.com*. Visit an independent bookstore, and try Barnes & Noble Booksellers, because the perfume of books is so intoxicating.

Go to the public library! Preschoolers enjoy exploring the huge shelves of books in a library. By three or four, children will learn to take interesting books off the shelves, then return them to appropriate bins to be re-shelved by librarians or volunteers.

A child's first library card represents momentous power! During the summer months, my cousin and I walked to the library twice a day. We borrowed three books each, read them all, and returned for six more books. Children's books are so short.

We read every book in the children's section, from *The Tale of Peter Rabbit* by Beatrix Potter (1902), to *The Cat in the Hat Comes Back* (1958) by Dr. Seuss.

Continue to buy hardback picture books for children to own. Good books can be found on sales counters in many bookstores, so start a family collection. Shelves of books in children's bedrooms or playrooms promotes a sense of belonging to the world of reading.

The children who develop the habit of finding books on interesting subjects, will become self-regulated learners. According to famous authors Agatha Christie and Eudora Welty, if young children fall in love with books, they may become the adults who write books.

# CHAPTER 5
# Communication for Preschool: 3 to 4 Years

American children attend preschool from the age of three to five. Many preschools are located in public schools, some in Head Start programs, and some in private childcare centers. In the year 2000, 600,000 U.S. teachers held jobs in preschools and kindergartens. They were often underpaid, and their work undervalued.

Most teachers know that their professional education will benefit children through an infinite variety of creative lessons. Sometimes children and their parents equate school with rote learning. But recognizing and reciting alphabet letters and numerals is only a small part of early childhood education.

Knowledgable teachers connect the alphabet and numerals to more complex kinds of learning, such as Botany, Geography, History, Mathematics, Science, and Zoology. Children love alphabet books that introduce them to concepts beyond reading and writing. Alphabet books have themes that appeal to different children, based on age, ethnicity, gender, or personal interests.

American children often enter preschool able to recognize many letters and numerals. Children feel proud to take part in school activities that build on their previous knowledge, so parents and other teachers discovered many ways to let a prepared environment support these pre-reading skills.

Talented adults can add letters and numerals to children's clothing, using thick fabric paint or iron-on transfers that are purchased at craft stores. Some clothing for children is manufactured with alphabet letters, numerals, or short phrases as decoration.

Single large alphabet letters can be placed on doors in children's homes, or near the door that leads to a hallway or a playground outside the classroom. Naming the letter and tracing it as they pass through the door will promote visual memory for alphabet letters, as well as provide large muscle movement of the arms.

An alphabet chart is usually displayed in a classroom. Photos or drawings of recognizable items help children remember the sounds of consonants and vowels. The letter A often stands for apple, C for cat, and K for kite. Alphabet charts reassure parents that this class supports literacy development.

Before alphabet charts were readily available, schoolchildren used hornbooks, the forerunners of alphabet books. Hornbooks were not books in the modern sense of the term. The word hornbook has been traced to the sixteenth century, when hornbooks were made of parchment protected by a sheet of transparent animal horn.

Hornbooks were primers in early America, teaching children the shapes and sounds of alphabet letters. Modern children like alphabet books that introduce concepts beyond reading and writing. Caregivers can read alphabet books before nap time or bed time. Children's first alphabet books should be formatted as sturdy Board Books to survive chewing, dropping, and drooling.

Alphabet books have been published for centuries, so used ones are easy to find. Several well-known children's authors and illustrators like Eric

Carle and Dr. Seuss have published alphabet books, but Jerry Pallotta is the master of this genre.

Jerry Pallotta wrote at least twenty-five alphabet books, including:

> *The Airplane Alphabet Book,*
> *The Beetle Alphabet Book,*
> *The Bird Alphabet Book,*
> *The Butterfly Alphabet Book,*
> *The Construction Alphabet Book,*
> *The Dinosaur Alphabet Book,*
> *The Flower Alphabet Book,*
> *The Frog Alphabet Book,*
> *The Icky Bug Alphabet Book,*
> *The Jet Alphabet Book,*
> *The Ocean Alphabet Book,* and
> *The Underwater Alphabet Book.*

Alphabet books can bridge the gap between familiarity and novelty. An alphabet book's educational value should widen children's horizons. Classic alphabet books, which often featured exotic animals like a *yak* or a *zebra*, still have value because animals of every kind attract young children.

As teachers gather materials for topical unit plans, they'll find alphabet books to enrich most of their lessons. The alphabet books below are listed by authors' last names.

## Insights R: Twenty-Four Alphabet Books

*LMNO Peas (The Peas Series)* (2014) by Keith Baker
*Animalia* (1987) by Graeme Base
*Alligator Alphabet* (2005) by Stella Blackstone, Stephanie Bauer
*Eric Carle's ABC* (2007) by Eric Carle

*Real Grands: From A to Z, Everything a Grandparent Can Be!* (2015) by
Deborah Carroll

*The Alphabet Book* (2005) by P. D. Eastman

*Eating the Alphabet: Fruits & Vegetables from A to Z* (1996) by Lois Ehlert

*Handsigns: A Sign Language Alphabet* (1993) by Kathleen Fain

*A is for Aloha* (1986) by Stephanie Feeney, Hella Hammid

*Alphabet Under Construction* (2002) by Denise Fleming

*Gyo Fujikawa's A to Z Picture Book* (1999) by Gyo Fujikawa

*A Apple Pie* (Illustrated) (2013) by Kate Greenaway

*Merriam-Webster's Alphabet Book* by Ruth Heller

*The Living Rain Forest: An Animal Alphabet Book* (2007) by Paul Kratter

*A Was Once an Apple Pie* (1994) by Edward Lear, Julie Lacome

*Chicka Chicka Boom Boom* (1989) by Bill Marten, Jr. and John Archambault

*Little Monster's Alphabet Book* (1978) by Mercer Mayer

*Yankee Doodle America: The Spirit of 1776 from A to Z* (2006) by
Wendell Minor

*Apple Pie ABC* (2011) by Alison Murray

*The Yucky Reptile Alphabet Book* (1989) by Jerry Pallotta and Ralph
Masiello

*The Underwater Alphabet Book* (1991) by Jerry Pallotta and Edgar
Stewart

*A Peaceable Kingdom: The Shaker Abecedarius* (1978) by Alice and
Martin Provensen

*M is for Maple: A Canadian Alphabet* (2001) by Mike Ulmer and
Melanie Rose

*Letter Tracing Book for Preschoolers: Learn to Write for Kids* (2017) by
Doris Wilson

Probably thousands of alphabet books were published over several
centuries. Some of them suggest physical exercises, as children try to
walk like the illustrated animals. Some inspire pretend play, as the
children dig like archeologists or construct like builders.

Preschoolers use pretend play to explore their future roles. They ambitiously try out new behaviors, but might annoy the adults around them. When my daughter Linnet was four, she tried to dig for dinosaur bones in our front lawn. Linnet was actually demonstrating initiative. In preschool she had learned that fossilized bones of dinosaurs were found by archeologists.

My husband had just planted new grass seed! Fortunately I was the parent who found Linnet digging up the lawn, so I moved her archeological dig to an old vegetable garden. I realized that Linnet was being inventive in an age-old way.

Researchers have demonstrated that the preschool years are a time of galloping development in communication skills. A time when parents and other teachers should examine children's environments to ensure that they promote language development.

The *Components of a Language-Rich Environment* are listed in Insights H, on page 23.

Sensible parents leave simple messages on mirrors and in lunch boxes to encourage preschoolers' reading. Providing art materials like textured paper, paste or glue, clay and dough, and non-toxic paints encourages preschool art.

To encourage communication skills, adults make language fun for preschoolers with call and response games, chanting, name games, rhyming, and silly songs. Beginners' card games will improve children's concentration and memory, abilities that are needed later for reading and writing.

Some adults might remember The Name Game, sung by Shirley Ellis in 1965. With different names, she sang *Jane, Jane, bow bane; Banana fanna, fow, fane; Fee, fie, mow mane; Jane!* Substituting various consonant sounds aids phonics learning.

The Hokey Pokey strengthens arms, legs and trunks. This game also promotes auditory skills, balance, concept development and directionality.

In early childhood, Circle Time, Group Time or Meeting Time provides an ideal opportunity to enhance children's development. Circle Games are so much fun the children won't suspect that they're good for them!

Who should play circle games? Two-year-olds are not ready for large group activities, but many three-year-olds will enjoy short circle games. All children can be invited to join the circle, but no child should be required to join. Circle Time should look like so much fun that most children voluntarily join the circle.

What types of circle games can children play? These games can involve call and response, dancing, imitation, improvisation, and singing. Circle games can be simple or complicated.

Adults can learn new circle games by observing teachers in different classrooms, or using a book that adds more children's activities to their repertoires. Soon the adults will begin to gather circle props, such as bells, hats, rhythm sticks, scarves and shakers.

Grown-ups also prepare for Circle Time by making illustrated index cards with the words to one circle song. Sometimes children like to be in charge, so each day a child can pick one card to choose a song for the class.

Teachers can cut out the words to twenty-four circle songs written on page 81. The children will choose favorites again and again, so rotate the song cards to keep interest high. Circle Games involve several senses to help children develop in the areas described in detail below.

# Insights S: Circle Games Support Development

1. Sensory Perception gives meaning to information taken in by the senses, such as hearing, seeing, smelling, tasting, and touching. Later, children will rely on their sense memory for writing composition.

2. Gross Motor Skills use large muscles for trunk, leg, and arm strength; balance and agility; ability to cross the midline; and bilateral coordination. Gross motor skills let children move about to gain information, and allow older children to sit for long periods of listening, reading, typing or writing.

3. Fine Motor Skills use small muscles of lips, tongue, eyes, and fingers. Fine motor strength, dexterity, and coordination are used for keyboard skills, for manuscript writing and for speech.

4. Language Skills include articulation, concept development, fluency, intonation, listening, rhyming, signing, singing, speaking, and vocabulary building. Writing composition is based on all earlier skills of communication.

5. Social Skills practiced at Circle Time involve cooperating in groups, courtesy, enjoying peer interaction, group identity, respecting people, sharing space, and turn-taking.

6. Emotional Skills include experiencing joy, pride, and satisfaction; recognizing and expressing emotions; empathizing with the emotions of others; and tolerating frustration. These *affective* skills are important tools for a satisfying adult life.

Many ethnic groups have traditional games that can enrich children's understanding of people's heritage. Adults can learn an activity from an unfamiliar culture, then teach it to the class.

Before adults try a new activity with children, they carefully consider what it will involve. Is this activity too easy or too hard for these children? What concepts will it teach? Circle Time should be both educational and enjoyable!

If babies are present at Circle Time, they are already developing some skills that they'll need later, for listening, talking, reading and writing. Certainly babies can't sing along with a group yet, but hearing other people singing is also valuable for language learning.

Gathering a group of young children for Circle Time is made easier with a routine. Adults often use the same signal every time, such as flashing the classroom lights or singing a familiar tune.

## Insights T: Announcing Circle Time

### A CLEAN-UP SONG

I like the way that Elena is cleaning,
I like the way that Ethan is cleaning,
I like the way that Tanya is cleaning,
We're almost ready for Circle Time!

### THE CIRCLE ROUND-UP SONG

Meeting, meeting, meeting,
Let's go to the meeting,
Circle, circle, circle, right now!
Welcome to our meeting,
We need you at our meeting,
Circle, circle, circle, right now!
(Sung to the melody of television's RAWHIDE theme)

# THE STEP RIGHT UP MARCH

It's Circle Time!
(Step right up, sit right down.)
It's talking time!
(Step right up, sit right down.)
It's listening time!
(Step right up, sit right down.)
It's meeting time right now!

In the late 19th century, Patty Smith Hill, an innovator in the Progressive Education Movement, taught kindergarten in Louisville, Kentucky. Patty Hill was acquainted with many of the prominent educators of that era and was influenced by their ideas.

Under G. Stanley Hall at Clark University, for example, Hill absorbed research on child psychology. At the University of Chicago, she studied John Dewey, who stated that children learn most effectively when they interact with their environment. Some summers she spent with Luther Gulick, who was elected president of the Playground Association of America in 1907.

Patty Smith Hill was credited with inventing several methods of teaching. For example, she recommended children's free play as educational. She also created very large building blocks to be used on the floor, where children could engage in dramatic play.

Patty's sister, Mildred J. Hill, composed music for the piano. The Hill sisters named each of Patty's kindergarten pupils when they sang *Good Morning to All* to Patty's class, a popular routine.

The melody and lyrics of *Good Morning to All* have been attributed to Patty and Mildred. But this was also disputed.

Using the same melody of *Good Morning to All,* in 1893 they wrote *Happy Birthday to You,* probably the most well-known song in English. In 1896 they published *Happy Birthday* in their book *Song Stories for the Kindergarten.* The lyrics and melody first appeared in print in 1912. Since then, *Happy Birthday* has been translated into over fifteen languages.

During Circle Time, a myriad of activities provide opportunities to improve children's development. If some children don't join the circle voluntarily, adults can give them a quiet activity like completing puzzles or building structures on a rug.

When these children see others enjoying Circle Time, they could choose to join the circle on their own. All people prefer to choose their own activities. They dislike feeling forced to do anything.

How do caregivers make Circle Time educational? The game *Head, Shoulders, Knees, and Toes* requires young children to name and touch several parts of their bodies. Rhythmic movements are practiced as they play this active game.

In the game *A My Name Is Alice,* children find matching vowel or consonant sounds. The first chant could be *"A my name is Alice and my boyfriend's name is Andy. We come from Alabama and we like apples."* The second verse might be *"B my name is Bobby and I come from Boston, with boxes of baked beans and butter."*

In the game *Telephone* children whisper to each other, trying to repeat the phrase traveling around the group. With hilarious and often intentional mistakes, the children are practicing their skills of auditory discrimination and creativity.

When performed in preschool, Circle Time songs can be very educational as well as entertaining. Insights U on page 81 provides the words for twenty-four popular circle songs.

## Insights U: Twenty-Four Circle Time Songs

### A TISKET, A TASKET

A Tisket, A Tasket,
A green and yellow basket.
I wrote a letter to my love,
And on the way I lost it.

I lost it! I lost it!
I lost my little letter.
A little laddie (lassie) picked it up,
And put it in his (her) pocket.

### ALLIGATOR PIE

Alligator Pie, Alligator Pie,
If I don't get some,
I think I'm gonna die.

Alligator Pie, Alligator Pie,
If I don't get some,
I think I'm gonna die.

Take away the green grass,
Take away the sky!
But please don't take away
My alligator pie!

### BLUEBIRD, BLUEBIRD

Bluebird, bluebird,
In and out my window,
Bluebird, bluebird,
In and out my window,
Bluebird, bluebird,

In and out my window,
Oh, bluebird*,
Are you tired?

*(Or insert a child's name as the bluebird)

## DID YOU EVER SEE A LASSIE? (or LADDIE?)

Did you ever see a lassie,
A lassie, a lassie?
Did you ever see a lassie,
Go this way and that?

Go this way and that way*,
Go this way and that way,
Did you ever see a lassie,
Go this way and that?

*(Children imitate motions of child in the center)

## RING AROUND THE ROSIE

Ring Around the Rosie,
A pocket full of posies,
Ashes, Ashes,
We all fall down!

## DOCTOR CATCHALL WITH HER SATCHEL

Doctor Catchall with her satchel,
Through the rain the doctor goes.
Splishy, splashy; Squishy, squashy,
She makes music with her toes.
Doctor! Doctor! I'm so sick!
Give me a rhythm pill,
Right quick!

# IT'S RAINING, IT'S POURING

It's raining, it's pouring;
The old man is snoring.
He went to bed and
He bumped his head,
And he couldn't get up
In the morning.

# DOWN AT THE STATION

Down at the station, *
Early in the morning,
See the little puffer bellies,
Standing in a row?
See the engine driver,
Pull the little lever,
Puff, Puff!
Toot, Toot!
Off we go!

*(Move in single file, hands on shoulders)

# THE HOKEY-POKEY

You put your right hand* in,
You take your right hand out,
You put your right hand in,
And you shake it all about!
You do the Hokey-Pokey,
And you turn yourself around,
That's what it's all about!

*(Left hand, right leg, elbow, belly, bottom, nose...)

## IF YOU'RE HAPPY AND YOU KNOW IT

If you're happy and you know it,
Clap your hands!*
If you're happy and you know it,
Clap your hands!
If you're happy and you know it,
And you really want to show it,
If you're happy and you know it,
Clap your hands!

*(Nod your head, flap your arms, lift your knees…)

## JUMPETY-JUMP POEM

Sweet little Tina*
Wants to jumpety-jump,
Jumpety-jump,
Jumpety-jump!

Sweet little Tina
Wants to jumpety-jump,
Now sweet little Tina
Wants to bow down low.

*(Substitute other children's names)

## GO IN AND OUT THE WINDOWS

(Children's clasped hands held up; one child weaves through)

Go In and Out the Windows,
Go In and Out the Windows,
Go In and Out the Windows,
As we have done before!

(Children crouch, lower arms; one child walks over them)

Go stepping over doorsteps,
Go stepping over doorsteps,
Go stepping over doorsteps,
As we have done before!

(The child walking around the circle taps next marcher.)

Go forth and choose a partner,
Go forth and choose a partner,
Go forth and choose a partner,
As we have done before!

## A WISE OLD OWL

A wise old owl lived in an oak.
The more he saw, the less he spoke.
The less he spoke, the more he heard.
Why can't we be like that wise old bird?

## HEAD, SHOULDERS, KNEES AND TOES

Head, shoulders, knees and toes, *
Knees and toes!
Head, shoulders, knees and toes,
Knees and toes!
And eyes and ears and a mouth and a nose!
Head, shoulders, knees and toes,
Knees and toes!

*(Children point to the body parts mentioned)

## LONDON BRIDGE

London Bridge is falling down,
Falling down, falling down.
London Bridge is falling down,
My fair lady.

Catch a kid and lock her (him) up,*
Lock her up, lock her up.
Catch a kid and lock her up,
My fair lady.

*(Two children hold hands, then catch another child)

## LITTLE RED CABOOSE

Little red caboose,*
Little red caboose,
Little red caboose behind the train.
Smoke stack on its back,
Going down the track,
Little red caboose behind the train.
Toot! Toot!

*(Children form train holding the waist of child in front of them)

## THE PEOPLE ON THE BUS

The people* on the bus go up and down,
Up and down, up and down.
The people on the bus go up and down,
All through the town.

* (The money on the bus goes "clink, clink, clink …")

(The driver on the bus says "Move on back …")
(The baby on the bus goes "Waa, Waa, Waa …")
(The mother on the bus says "Sh, Sh, Sh...")
(A man on the bus says "Take my seat…")

## I'M A LITTLE TEAPOT

I'm a little teapot,
Short and stout.
Here is my handle, *
Here is my spout.
When I get all steamed up,
Hear me shout.
Just TIP me over,
And pour me out!

I'm a very special pot,
It's true.
Let me show,
What I can do.
I can change my handle,
And my spout.
Just TIP me over,
And pour me out!

*(Place one hand on a hip and make a spout with the other)

## MISS MARY MACK

Miss Mary Mack, Mack, Mack,
All dressed in black, black, black,
With silver buttons, buttons, buttons,
All down her back, back, back.

She asked her mother, mother, mother,
For fifty cents, cents, cents,
To see the elephant, elephant, elephant,
Jump over the fence, fence, fence.

He jumped so high, high, high,
He reached the sky, sky, sky,
And he didn't come back, back, back,
Till the fourth of July! Lie! Lie!

## MARY HAD A LITTLE LAMB

Mary had a little lamb,
Little lamb, little lamb,
Mary had a little lamb,
Its fleece was white as snow.

Everywhere that Mary went,
Mary went, Mary went,
Everywhere that Mary went
The lamb was sure to go.

## OPEN, SHUT THEM

Open, shut them, Open, shut them,
Give a little clap! (CLAP)
Open, shut them, Open, shut them,
Put them in your lap.

Sneak them, creep them,
Creep them, sneak them,
Right up to your chin!
Open wide your little mouth,
But do not let them in!

# THIS TRAIN IS BOUND FOR GLORY

This train is bound for glory, this train.*
This train is bound for glory, this train.
This train is bound for glory,
Won't take none, but the good and holy,
This train is bound for glory, this train.

* (This train is speeding up now, this train …
Hang on tight as it flies by now…)

(This train is going slowly, this train …
Wave to friends as it slips by, now…)

## PAW-PAW PATCH

Where Oh where is sweet little Jenny? *
Where Oh where is sweet little Jenny?
Where Oh where is sweet little Jenny?
Way down yonder, in the Paw-Paw patch!

Pickin' up Paw-Paws, Put 'em in her pocket,
Pickin' up Paw-Paws, Put 'em in her pocket,
Pickin' up Paw-Paws, Put 'em in her pocket,
Way down yonder in the Paw-Paw patch!

* (Change child's name; Children mime the words to the song)

# WE'RE GOING TO KENTUCKY

We're going to Kentucky,
We're going to the fair,
To see a Señorita (or Handsome Hombre)
With flowers in her (his) hair.

Oh, shake it, shake it, shake it,
Shake it if you can,
Shake it like a milk shake,
And do it once again!

Oh, rhumba to the bottom,
And rhumba to the top,
And turn around and turn around,
Until you make a STOP!

There are many children's games for both large and small groups. These include *Dominoes*; *Duck, Duck, Goose*; *Hide and Seek*; *Mother May I*; *Musical Chairs* and *Simon Says*. Such games foster gross-motor skills, fine-motor skills, and language development.

When adults play alphabet games like *The Name Game*, they increase children's knowledge of the encoding and decoding processes. In the game *Scrabble for Juniors,* children match pictures to words, and find alphabet letters that spell words.

When young children understand letter-sound correspondence, they can draw lines between the pictures of objects and the alphabet letters representing the beginning sounds of those objects.

The Learning Company is a software company founded forty years ago in Palo Alto, CA. Now owned by Houghton Mifflin Harcourt, it promotes reading and writing skills, like letter recognition, letter-sound correspondence, and beginning phonics.

In 1983 The Learning Company designed Reader Rabbit, a game aimed at children from preschool through second grade. ClueFinders was released in 1998, for third through sixth grade. More information is found at the website: *learningcompany.com.*

Some computer software uses cartoons to hold children's attention. Computer games that encourage creativity are more valuable.

Sometimes computer software and workbooks can make reading and writing seem dull or too complicated. Some so-called aids are not teaching but are really drilling, or testing what the children already learned. Success with drills, however, could be affirming, especially when skills are new to children.

Around 1937, the first programmable computer was invented by Konrad Zuse in his parents' living room. Zuse created an electro-mechanical binary computer, the world's first functional computer.

In the 1970s Steve Jobs was a pioneer in the microcomputer revolution. With Steve Wozniak, he founded Apple Incorporated, a multinational company that designed computer software.

In 1975, Bill Gates was the principal founder of Microsoft, the largest software company in the world. He was the best-known entrepreneur in the insurgence of personal computers.

Computers were soon a necessary tool for writers. But some of the world's most famous authors lived before the age of computers. They wrote by hand or used manual typewriters.

William Shakespeare died in 1564, Jane Austen in 1817, Charles Dickens in 1870, Emily Dickinson in 1886, Mark Twain in 1910, Virginia Woolf in 1941, Langston Hughes in 1967, Martin Luther King Jr. in 1968, Agatha Christie in 1976. These authors didn't have computers when they wrote their unforgettable works.

Most children learn to read and write without a computer in any language-rich surroundings. Insights H on page 23 lists the many components of a language-rich environment for children.

What children need to develop literacy is an adult who will respond to their interest in reading and writing. Fortunate children have experiences that facilitate language development and feed their imaginations. These include conversing with adults, listening to adults read aloud, and watching their own words written and read back to them.

In *Tom: The Unknown Tennessee Williams* by Lyle Leverich, (1995) America's great playwright is quoted. "My sister and I were gloriously happy. We sailed paper boats in washtubs of water, cut lovely paper dolls out of huge mail-order catalogs, kept two white rabbits under the back porch, baked mud pies in the sun upon the front walk, climbed up and slid down the big wood pile …"

Before he became a world-famous writer, Tennessee Williams played like most children did before computers were invented. Adults can give children valuable educational opportunities by encouraging play with everyday objects.

To promote eye-hand coordination and writing, adults can foster fine-motor development in increasingly complicated ways. Children with physical disabilities could still become skillful writers. They will rely on intellectual skills for composition.

The physicist Stephen Hawking was a famous writer who used technology to compensate for his fine-motor deficits. In *A Brief History of Time: From the Big Bang to Black Holes* (1988), Hawking shone a light on cosmology for the non-scientist.

Adequate language development is crucial for writers. Adults should talk to children about their ongoing fine-motor activities and take dictation about children's arts and crafts.

Building with large and small blocks, cutting or ripping paper, drawing with pencils, pens or markers, learning to crochet or knit, painting, sewing with a needle and thread, and squeezing dough and clay are some fine-motor activities that will improve children's coordination.

Water Play is a versatile fine-motor activity. Water play can take place in the bathtub, at the beach, in a large plastic bin, in a sink, in a swimming pool, or at a water table.

Playing in water can involve blowing bubbles, dripping, measuring, pouring and splashing. Children can even *paint* with water, using brushes of several sizes, and making marks that disappear quickly from the sides of buildings or sidewalks.

Tools for water play to be found around the house include funnels, measuring cups, pitchers, plastic mixing bowls, sponges and turkey basters. Many objects could be added to a bin of water, including a doll that needs a bath, doll clothes or socks to wash.

As the adults around them comment on children's water play, they can introduce concepts like absorb, dissolve, empty and full. Discovering which objects will sink and which ones float is an experiment that involves concepts of physics.

Playing with water will cool children in the summer and is always soothing to their spirits. A warm bath filled with the right toys can provide up to 45 minutes of educational water play for children. But wise adults never leave children unattended near water. Drowning is both quick and tragic!

Another valuable fine-motor activity involves clay or dough. Using these manipulatives, children can cut, flatten, imprint, poke, pound, squeeze, or stretch the material. Making balls of dough, pancakes, or ropes uses both arms in bilateral integration.

Several types of modeling clay can be purchased in craft stores, but a batch of dough also can be made up at home. Insights V on page 95, provides Six Easy Art Recipes including two for play dough.

Much useful information about play dough can be found on the Internet. Commercial Play-Doh® Fun factories will interest older children, but many tools for dough are found around the house. These include cookie cutters, emery boards, forks, a garlic press, knives, plastic containers, prickly hair rollers, scissors, spoons, straws, and wooden spools.

Sand Play is another time-tested way to promote fine-motor, intellectual, and tactile development in children. Sand, dry rice and dry beans are tiny solids that act like liquids because they can be poured and measured.

Transferred from hand to hand, dry rice and beans run right through little fingers like water. Some of the same equipment used for water play will work for sand play.

Bins of beans, rice or sand must be monitored by adults. Algae, insects and mold can grow in the bins, but they'll last for years if kept away from moisture. Water tables and plastic bins should be emptied regularly, and cleaned by grown-ups with a mild chlorine bleach and water solution.

For large jobs, use a solution of ½ cup bleach with one gallon of water. For individual toys, use 1¼ teaspoons bleach in a cup of water. Pre-wash surfaces with detergent and water, then sanitize with the bleach and water solution for five minutes. Allow treated objects to air dry.

A sandbox in the yard must be kept covered to keep cats out of it. Sand will scratch some toys like metal trucks or plastic dolls, so adults should monitor these toys, removing any damaged ones. Keeping tools clean and throwing out damaged toys demonstrates to children a respect for their belongings.

Traditionally, parents saved children's paper crafts for years, taking pride in their children's creativity. Adults can encourage children to create paper crafts at home, including paper chains, paper-bag costumes, paper-bag puppets, and self-decorated wrapping paper. Some art materials can be made at home, using recipes listed below.

## Insights V: Six Easy Art Recipes

COOKED PLAY DOUGH

2 cups flour
1 cup salt
2 tablespoons cooking oil
3 drops food color in 2 cups water
Mix and cook on medium heat
Cool before use
If sticky, knead with flour

NO-COOK PLAY DOUGH

2 cups flour
1 cup salt
2 tablespoons salad oil
2 drops color in 1 cup water
Mix all ingredients
Add flour if sticky

COOKED CRAFT PASTE

Boil 1 cup water
Add ½ cup flour
Reduce heat to low
Stir until thick and shiny
Allow paste to cool before use

NO-COOK CRAFT PASTE

1 cup flour
½ cup water
Mix until creamy
Store in an airtight container

COOKED FINGER PAINT

1 cup flour
2 drops food coloring
in ¾ cup water
Mix on low heat, until thick as ketchup

NO-COOK FINGER PAINT

1 cup flour
½ cup water w/3 drops of color
Mix until thick as ketchup

# MORE ART PROJECTS

To create textured signs, young children can paste dry pasta over their names printed on cardboard by an adult. When preschoolers pick up individual pieces of dry pasta, they are exercising the pincer grip, to be used later to hold brushes, crayons, pencils and pens for drawing and writing.

Arranged as a collage, magazine pictures can be pasted on colored paper for wall decorations, or as presents for family and friends. Children will be able to cut images from magazines more easily if the pictures are first outlined by an adult with a thick marker. Making arrangements of pictures as collages can be useful practice for making arrangements of words as written compositions.

A fringe snipped around a rolled paper cone resembles the petals of a flower when the edge of a dull knife is used to curl the petals. Paper dolls and snowflakes are fascinating creations that surprise us when unfolded, just as written compositions often surprise authors with new meanings when they are re-read.

Children can use fingernails, knuckles, or palms in finger paint. If finger paint is used on a serving tray or a cookie sheet, clean-up will be easy in the sink. Sometimes shaving cream is smeared around on plastic trays or tabletops for an especially easy clean-up. But don't use shaving cream with children young enough to touch their eyes, because soap stings!

Painting can involve large or small brushes, sponges, straws or other tools. Painting at an easel is different than painting on a flat surface like a table, or using paint like ink to print with potatoes or sponges. Two children can paint on opposite sides of an upright sheet of clear plastic to practice interactive composition.

When clothing was created at home, learning to sew was part of most children's education. Quilting, tapestry and weaving were decorative and useful arts. In this era of technology and mass marketing, these experiences with fabric and needle must be organized by knowledgable parents and other teachers.

Colorful pieces of yarn, one end stiffened with glue or tape, make a safe needle and thread for young children. Stringing pasta or breakfast cereal with large openings aids fine-motor skills.

Patterning is practiced by stringing different shapes or colors. When children plan their patterns as crayon drawings, they are recording their thoughts, a precursor to writing.

Yarn can be used to embroider on sewing cards. Colorful cardboard or wooden sewing cards are sold at craft stores, but sewing cards can be created of plastic foam trays collected from grocery stores. To make a sewing card, poke a clean foam tray with a knitting needle, on marker lines drawn by an adult or a child.

## Insights W: Fine-Motor Materials And Equipment

> Big and Small Boxes
> Building Blocks of Cardboard or Wood
> Chalk and Crayons
> Clay and Dough
> Dried Rice and Beans
> Glue and Paste
> Paint Brushes
> Pegboards
> Pencils, Pens, Markers
> Scissors
> Several Types of Paper
> Simple Jigsaw Puzzles

Staplers
String and Yarn
Toy Cars and Trucks

Any use of children's fine-motor skills will benefit future writing ability. Playing with commercial manipulatives like interlinking plastic rings, interlocking bricks, nesting cups, table blocks, or tiny vehicles can enhance children's eye-hand coordination.

When treats are picked up one at a time with only fingertips, even snacks like dry cereal, nuts or raisins can provide practice for the pincer grip and strengthen the fingers.

# CHAPTER 6
## Communication for Kindergarten: 5 to 6 Years

Five-year-old children are capable communicators. Five-year-olds typically speak in sentences that average five words, such as "I do not like dogs." When children are six, their sentences average six words in length. "Dogs are scary because they bite."

Children usually enter kindergarten when they are five years old. Their fine-motor skills allow them to make recognizable objects of clay or dough, and to draw a person with 3 to 4 body parts.

Six-year-old children draw people with 5 to 7 body parts. They also begin to read common signs like STOP and EXIT, but reading instruction is reserved for the first grade.

Many American children attend public school kindergarten. The original Kindergarten, or a garden where children can grow and flourish, was named in 1840 by the pioneering German educator, Friedrich Froebel.

Froebel was born in central Germany to affluent parents, but his mother died before he was a year old. He was raised by an uncle who advised Friedrich to obtain higher education.

Friedrich Froebel has been called education's most influential reformer. His studies in mathematics and the sciences, including botany, geology and physics, showed him natural patterns and cycles that informed his philosophy of education. Froebel believed that activities like dancing, gardening and telling stories promoted children's self-initiated education.

To encourage children's activities, Froebel designed toys shaped like cubes, cylinders and spheres, intended to stimulate children's thinking as they play. These froebelgaben, or gifts, were to be used as educational puzzles and art materials in schools.

Inspired by Friedrich Froebel, Caroline Pratt created Unit Blocks early in the 20th century. Unit Blocks remain standard equipment in programs for young children.

These sturdy wooden blocks are accurately sized in mathematical ratios of 1:2:4. Unit Blocks are open-ended equipment that support children's mathematics learning and their creativity.

In 1913 Lucy Sprague Mitchell was a founder of Bank Street College of Education and the Bureau of Educational Experiences, both in New York City. The bureau sponsored Caroline Pratt's Play School, which nurtured the abilities of the whole child.

Before teachers can affect children's optimal development, they need to nurture their own growth. Bank Street College is known for inspiring early childhood specialists and famous authors like Margaret Wise Brown and Edith Thacher Hurd.

Margaret Wise Brown wrote 150 children's books, famously *The Runaway Bunny* (1942) and *Goodnight Moon* (1947). Edith Thacher Hurd published 75 children's books, among them *Stop, stop* (1961) and *The Mother Chimpanzee* (1978). Her husband Clement Hurd illustrated some books for both authors.

Tomie dePaola created more than 260 children's books, including *Nana Upstairs and Nana Downstairs* (1973), *The Cloud Book* (1975), *The Popcorn Book* (1978), *Strega Nona* (1979), and *Adelita: A Mexican Cinderella Story* (2004).

Communication also can be supported in kindergarten by holding a regular Speakers Circle. This is a class activity that supports language development for later reading and writing.

A Speakers Circle uses a prop to focus the children's attention. A laminated, multicolored paper circle works well. Holding this circle, an adult introduces a topic, models a short comment, and passes the circle to next person in the Speakers Circle.

Holidays like The Fourth of July, Halloween, Thanksgiving, and Valentine's Day can be discussed in a Speakers Circle. Do all families celebrate this holiday? Insights X suggests other topics.

## Insights X: Ten Topics For A Speakers Circle

1. What's your favorite breakfast cereal?

2. What's your favorite fruit or vegetable?

3. What pizza toppings do you like or dislike?

4. Describe a favorite coat, hat, shirt, shoes, or socks.

5. Where do you want to go on a vacation? Why?

6. What type of lessons do you want? Ballet, Karate, Yoga ...

7. Which actors, animals, sports stars or writers are interesting?

8. Name a job or career that's interesting to you.

9. Name a job or career that is not interesting. Why not?

10. Name your favorite holiday. Why is it special?

When children begin to read, they like to use this new ability. Children deserve high-quality reading materials, especially books that are both educational and entertaining. Adults can ask a librarian or a teacher to pick age-appropriate books for a child, or they can find impressive books from their own childhood.

Theodor Seuss Geisel became a key figure in literature with his first book written for children, *And To Think That I Saw It On Mulberry Street,* published in 1937. Known under pen names as Dr. Seuss and Theo LeSieg, (Geisel spelled backwards) this popular author and illustrator was innovative in the 20th century.

## Insights Y: Thirty-Five Books For Young Readers

*Skyfire* (1990) by Frank Asch
*Happy Birthday Moon* (2005) by Frank Asch
*Bears on Wheels* (1969) by Stan and Jan Berenstain
*He Bear She Bear* (1974) by Stan and Jan Berenstain
*The Children of Green Knowe* (1975) by L. M. Boston
*Treasure of Green Knowe* (1978) by L. M. Boston
*Sailor Boy Jig* (2002) by Margaret Wise Brown
*Sneakers, the Seaside Cat* (2003) by Margaret Wise Brown
*My Very First Book of Colors* (2005) by Eric Carle
*My Very First Book Of Words* (2006) by Eric Carle
*Are You My Mother?* (1960) by P. D. Eastman
*The Best Nest* (1968) by P. D. Eastman
*Gone-Away Lake* (1957) by Elizabeth Enright
*Return to Gone-Away* (1961) by Elizabeth Enright

*Choose Your Own Autobiography* (2014) by Neil Patrick Harris
*The Magic Misfits* (2017) by Neil Patrick Harris
*Benny and Penny in Lights Out!* (2015) by Geoffrey Hayes
*A Poor Excuse for a Dragon* (2011) by Geoffrey Hayes
*The Grimm Conclusion* (2013) by Adam Gidwitz
*The Creature of the Pines* (2018) by Adam Gidwitz
*Jog, Frog, Jog* (1984) by Barbara Gregorich
*My Friend Goes Left* (1996) by Barbara Gregorich
*The Enormous Turnip* (1998) by Ladybird Books
*Ten Apples Up On Top* (1961) by Theo LeSeig
*The Eye Book* (1968) by Theo LeSeig and Roy McKie
*Frog and Toad Together* (1971) by Arnold Lobel
*Mouse Tales* (1972) by Arnold Lobel
*Hand, Hand, Fingers, Thumb* (1969) by Al Perkins, Eric Gurney
*The Nose Book* (1970) by Al Perkins and Roy Mckie
*Harry Potter and the Philosopher's Stone* (2002) by J. K. Rowling
*Harry Potter and the Chamber of Secrets* (2016) by J. K. Rowling
*Hop on Pop* (1963) by Dr. Seuss
*Green Eggs and Ham* (1960) by Dr. Seuss
*I Don't Like Peas* (1993) by Marie Vinje
*The Cat That Sat* (1993) by Marie Vinje

Sharing favorite books will bring children together. Wise teachers provide time and space for friendships to develop in classrooms and on the playground. Knowing that peer friendships enhance learning, teachers recognize that children's chatter is beneficial. Insights C on page 10 lists fourteen theorists who emphasize children's relationships.

As parents and other teachers realize, six-year-olds are individuals with a variety of interests and strengths. In my kindergarten in New York State, one little boy entered school reading at a fifth-grade level. In the same class, another boy rarely spoke or looked at books, but he built elaborate block buildings and constructed a house of snow with many rooms and tunnels.

Young children's skills are very diverse. They demonstrate a variety of abilities, based on their varied interests.

Howard Gardner, an American developmental psychologist, proposed a cognitive theory of multiple intelligences that can explain this diversity among same-age children (Insights Z). Gardner's famous book, *Frames of Mind: The Theory of Multiple Intelligences*, was published in 1983. Gardner said there was a biological basis for at least eight different ways children process information.

Howard Gardner theorized that human intelligence was not a single entity, but was made up of several independent factors. While most children have some abilities in all areas of intelligence, a small number of children excel in one or more areas.

## Insights Z: Gardner's Eight Types Of Intelligence

1. LINGUISTIC

2. LOGICAL-MATHEMATICAL

3. MUSICAL

4. SPATIAL

5. BODILY-KINESTHETIC

6. NATURALISTIC

7. INTERPERSONAL

8. INTRAPERSONAL

Linguistic Intelligence is the ability to understand and to use spoken and written language. People with high linguistic intelligence express themselves effectively in speech and in writing. They also learn to understand and to speak foreign languages rather easily.

In Howard Gardner's terms, authors, lawyers, newscasters, poets, and translators would have high linguistic intelligence.

Logical-Mathematical Intelligence gives people excellent skills of logic and an affinity for mathematics and reasoning. According to these folks, simple logic will provide the solution to every problem. They believe in applying reason and detecting patterns to arrive at solutions. Professionals that require logical-mathematical intelligence include computer scientists, math teachers and statisticians.

Musical Intelligence is the ability to easily recognize sounds and tones. Also called Musicality, it's a sensitivity to and a talent for music. Those with high musical intelligence can recognize and reproduce differing pitch, rhythm and harmony. People with musical intelligence could become choir directors, composers, musicians, music teachers, songwriters or vocalists.

Spatial Intelligence provides the ability to solve spatial problems like navigation and visualization of objects from different angles. Gardner's definition suggests that airplane pilots, architects, astronauts, building designers, mechanics, race car drivers, surgeons and taxi drivers all need excellent spatial intelligence.

Bodily-Kinesthetic Intelligence is defined as people's control of their bodily motions, and their ability to handle objects with skill.

Gardner indicated that this includes a sense of timing, knowledge of the goal of a physical action, and the ability to train bodily responses. People with high bodily-kinesthetic intelligence are good at physical activities including acting, athletics, building, dancing, gymnastics, and physical therapy.

Naturalistic Intelligence deals with the natural world, especially with visual and observational skills that discriminate between shapes, smells, textures and other qualities. Naturalistic Intelligence helped hunter-gatherers identify the plants and animals that were edible. This intelligence is found in parts of the brain that recognize patterns, make subtle connections, and discriminate among objects.

Both John Muir and Frederick Law Olmsted had high naturalistic intelligence, allowing them to explore their country and to design extensive national and local park systems.

Interpersonal Intelligence refers to how skilled a person is at understanding people. Those with this strength are aware of other people's feelings and motives, so they can manage relationships and negotiate conflicts. Professions that are a natural fit for people with interpersonal intelligence include acting, diplomacy, politics, psychology, sales, social work, teaching and therapy.

Intrapersonal Intelligence is the ability to be self-aware and to practice self-reflection. People with high intrapersonal intelligence reflect on their strengths and appreciate their feelings and motivations. Their self-knowledge and critical thinking makes them suited to professions such as authors of autobiographies, philosophers, psychiatrists and scientists.

A possible ninth intelligence, Existential Intelligence, is also referred to as spiritual intelligence. Existential Intelligence is an ability to conceptualize deeper or larger questions about human existence. "Why are human beings on earth?" "Why do they die?"

Those with Existential Intelligence think about the meaning of life, the purpose of birth and death, the existence of consciousness, and other fundamental questions of existence.

Howard Gardner did not fully confirm or endorse this intelligence. He did explain that people with Existential Intelligence are "Individuals who exhibit the proclivity to pose and ponder questions about life, death, and ultimate realities."

In *Intelligence Reframed: Multiple Intelligences for the 21st Century* (1999) Gardner reports on the evolution of his innovative theory and on recent revisions.

# CHAPTER 7

# Communication Exercises

Like any muscles, the writing muscles are built slowly, and they take proper nutrition and exercise to build. That's only a metaphor, but writing does require intellect or mental power, physically located in the brain. Building a writer requires the healthy nutrition provided by articles, books, journals and other written material. Appropriate writing exercises for each age group are also valuable.

There are many writing prompts that parents and other teachers can use with the children in their care. At many bookstores and libraries, adults will find workbooks with additional writing exercises. Over twenty examples of writing exercises are listed below, but don't stop with these suggestions!

## WRITING EXERCISES

### 1. FAVORITE PEOPLE

Ask children to name their favorite people. Take dictation from children to fill in the blanks on prepared papers. For each person named, the children complete these sentences:

I like (this person) because _____.
I want to (do something or go somewhere) with _____.

The sentences can be glued to drawing paper so children can draw a picture for each sentence. These make a wonderful bulletin board with captions that can be read by the children themselves.

## 2. MINING FOR INTERESTS

Ask children to name stories to hear, movies to see, or books to read aloud in school this year. The children's ideas can be displayed on a bulletin board titled: OUR INTERESTS NOW.

## 3. TIC-TAC-TOE

Copy four simple game boards for each child, using a ruler to draw two lines down and two lines across, to get the games started quickly. Two children play on one board. They take turns printing an O or an X in a square formed by the lines.

The goal is to place three of the same symbols in a line on the board: horizontally, vertically, or diagonally. The children should alternate being the first person to place an X or an O. They will rarely discover a strategy that consistently wins, but they'll enjoy printing the alphabet letters X and O!

## 4. FIRST LETTERS TO WRITE

When teaching young children to print, notice that a few alphabet letters are legible whether printed backwards or forwards:

(A, H, i, I, l, M, o, O, t, T, v, V, w, W, x, X)

Most letters (except H, I, o, O, x, and X) are not the same when written upside down. Directionality confuses young children, so they often reverse letters. Understanding the concepts *left* and *right* usually doesn't develop before children are six-years-old.

In one writing exercise, an adult prints a FIRST LETTER on one line of a piece of paper. After seeing how the letter is formed, the children practice writing that letter across a line.

## 5. FIRST WORDS TO WRITE

When teaching FIRST WORDS TO WRITE, use words that are legible if children reverse any letters. Use this list of first words to write: HAM, HAT, Hi! Hill, HOT, I, ill, MA'AM, MAT, mill, MOM, Moo! OH! OHIO, Ox, till, TOM, too, tow, will, WOW.

To create writing exercises using these first words, fold lined paper so that one word can head each column. Then children can copy each word several times under your model.

## 6. FIRST PHRASES TO WRITE

With simple words written in upper-case letters, meaningful PHRASES can be written by young children. C, D, E, L, and S require understanding of directionality, but most six-years-olds can copy the following phrases.

> WOW! HAM! MMM...
> TOO HOT, MOM!
> I LOVE MOM. MOM LOVES ME!
> I LOVE DAD. DAD LOVES ME!
> I LOVE SIS. SIS LOVES ME!
> I LOVE BRO. BRO LOVES ME!
> I LOVE THE CAT IN THE TALL HAT!

## 7. WHAT I LOVE TO EAT

On drawing paper folded vertically in three parts, children draw a food they love in each column: *apples, bananas, chicken, hamburgers, hot dogs, ice cream, pizza...* After children name the item, an adult labels that favorite food. Then children dictate one sentence the grown-up writes on the bottom of the page.

> I love to eat fried chicken.
> I don't like peas and carrots.
> Apples and peanut butter taste great!
> I like mashed potatoes.
> I hate squash and I hate spinach.

## 8. WISH LISTS

Children dictate several sentences starting with I WISH… These sentences will create a prose poem, such as the example printed below. After the poems are printed or typed on the bottom of a sheet of drawing paper, the children can illustrate them.

### WISHING POEM

> I wish I had a cat,
> I wish I could fly,
> I wish I were a witch,
> I wish I could fly on a broomstick,
> I wish I could do magic like Harry Potter,
> I wish it was my birthday,
> I wish that beds could really fly.

## 9. DIFFERENT ANIMALS

A piece of drawing paper is folded in half. After the children see several photos of animals, they draw two animals on their paper: one that they like, and one that they dislike. An adult labels each animal, such as a *bear, bird, cat, cow, dog, duck, frog, horse, lion, lizard, owl, penguin, tiger, skunk, spider,* or *swan.*

Take children's dictation for their comments under each picture:

I have a dog that licks me.
Bears are very big.
My sister has a bird in a cage.
Cats and dogs can be nice pets.
I saw scary snakes at the zoo.
A deer ran into our car.
All the dinosaurs are dead.
A skunk is very stinky.

## 10. REFLECTIONS OF NAMES

An adult folds drawing paper lengthwise in half. A line is drawn with a ruler in the middle six inches on the fold. On that line, children print their first names with a very bright or dark crayon. Then the children decorate their names with lighter crayons.

Using a warm iron when the children are not in the room, the adult melts the crayon wax on the folded paper, creating a lighter reflection under the line. NAME REFLECTIONS make a lovely decoration on a bulletin board, to provide reading practice as children read their classmates' names.

## 11. POETRY ABOUT FEELINGS

Create a FEELINGS CHART with simple line drawings of these 10 emotional states: *afraid, angry, disgusted, friendly, happy, lonely, proud, sad, scary, surprised.* Each child chooses one emotion as the title of a poem or short prose piece, and writes about that feeling.

These are posted on a bulletin board, or copied for all the children.

HAPPY by Laura, age 6
Tomorrow is a day closer
To my birthday.
When it is my birthday,
I will be really happy!
My birthday is in June.

HAPPY by Jeff, age 6
Happy is having a hamster,
Happy is having a good friend.
Happy is being at home,
Happy is having a good mom.

## 12. CREATING KID'S FIRST BOOKS

Children dictate words to create small books that they'll illustrate. An adult prints the title and author of the book on a construction-paper cover, using newsprint or typing paper for the pages. Both covers and pages will be cut into an interesting shape, then assembled and stapled along one side.

Small books can be created for individual alphabet letters, making covers cut in the shape of the letter, such as O WORDS, T WORDS, or L WORDS. Children draw an item beginning with that letter on each page, and adults write the dictated word.

The pages in MY WHEEL BOOK are round. The children's drawings are labeled by an adult on the bottom of each page: *A car has wheels, A bike has wheels, A bus has wheels, A tricycle has wheels, A truck has wheels, A wagon has wheels...*

SUNNY DAYS is also a round book, and could have pointed parts to suggest rays of the sun. For each page children dictate an action to complete the starter ON A SUNNY DAY: *I might get sunburned, I play ball, I go to a beach, I wear a wide hat, I can't see clouds ...*

RAINY DAYS is a blue construction paper book cut in the shape of a drop of water. The starter is ON A RAINY DAY: *I can watch the rain, I play in the rain, I collect rain in a cup, I play indoors, I look for a rainbow, I splash in the puddles ...*

THE RAINBOW has a color name printed at the bottom of each page. Children draw items like BLUE jeans, BROWN cocoa, a GREEN tree, GREY clouds, PINK cotton candy, PURPLE grapes, ORANGE carrots, a RED apple, VIOLET flowers, YELLOW sun, WHITE clouds.

## 13. DESCRIBING YOUR DAY

Children describe their day in detail, beginning "Today was a (*cold, dull, exciting, great, happy, hard, hot, loud, maddening, quiet, rainy, sad, silly, stormy, terrible, unusual* or *wonderful*) day."

Children's descriptions can be dictated, or older children can write their own descriptions with some help for spelling.

### A GREAT DAY!
by Julia, age 6

Today was a great day! Except for library. I had Tap. It was fun! Linnet is sick at home. Sometimes I wish I did not have my sister. My name is Julia. I have a friend named Krista. I play with her all the time. It is fun. We usually stay inside. We do things with beads. I do lots of things in my life. They're always fun!

## 14. COPYING POETRY

Children copy and illustrate significant short poems. This activity can provide examples of excellent composition, as well as reading and writing practice. Start with the following three poems:

### THE SECRET SITS
by Robert Frost

We dance round in a ring and suppose,
But the Secret sits in the middle and knows.

## ANONYMOUS NURSERY RHYME

Girls and boys come out to play,
The moon doth shine as bright as day.
Leave your supper, and leave your sleep,
And come with your playfellows into the street.
Come with a whoop, come with a call,
Come with good will, or come not at all.
Up the ladder and down the wall,
A halfpenny roll will serve us all.
You find milk, and I'll find flour,
And we'll have a pudding in half an hour.

## BROOMS
by Dorothy Aldis

On stormy days
When the wind is high
Tall trees are brooms
Sweeping the sky.
They swish their branches
In buckets of rain,
And swash and sweep it
Blue again.

## 15. FANTASY VEHICLES

A book about a fantasy vehicle is read to the class. These include *The Little Engine That Could* by Watty Piper, *The Polar Express* by Chris Van Allsburg, and *The Twenty-One Balloons* by William Pène du Bois. Then children describe their own fantasy vehicle. This activity can introduce the writing reminders: Who, What, Where, When, Why and How.

# FIVE FANTASY VEHICLE WRITING PROMPTS

1. What does your fantasy vehicle look like? Size and color?

2. Is your fantasy vehicle fast or slow?

3. Where does it go? In the air? On the street? Under water?

4. Who owns the fantasy vehicle? Who is the driver?

5. Are there passengers in your vehicle? Who are they?

## 16. MY BOOK ABOUT ME

The children will write their autobiographies. First, an adult talks about the differences between an *autobiography* and a *biography*.

David A. Adler wrote many biographies for children, including *A Picture Book of Thomas Alva Edison* and *A Picture Book of Rosa Parks*. Jean Fritz, also a productive biographer, wrote *The Double Life of Pocahontas*, and *Alexander Hamilton: The Outsider.*

After taking dictation from children, an adult fills in the blanks in MY BOOK ABOUT ME. Then the completed autobiography is stapled or otherwise bound.

# MY BOOK ABOUT ME

By _____ Date _____

1.  I am _____ years old. My birthday is_____

    _____

2.  In my family are my _____

    _____

3.  Here are my friends _____

4.  Here is my favorite pet _____

5.  My favorite foods are _____

    _____

6.  I hate this food _____

7.  My favorite treat is_____

8.  Here's how I have fun. I'm _____

9.  My home address is _____

10. This is the title of a great book _____

Children with and without hearing impairment, can use American Sign Language to extend early communication. Adults use books like *Baby Signs* by Joy Allen (2008), and *Handsigns: A Sign Language Alphabet* by Kathleen Fain (1993), to support early language learning.

Infants communicate with their whole bodies, wriggling with pleasure or thrashing about with frustration. When toddlers are ten to eighteen months, they begin to use some spoken words, eye movements and hand signals to communicate.

My one-year-old granddaughter could ask for her favorite song by signing *banana*.

### A SONG ABOUT FRUIT
by Theresa M. Sull

Oh, give me some fruit,
I don't give a hoot!
But my very favorite fruit
Is banana.
An orange is okay,
Or an apple a day,
But my favorite,
Absolutely
Is banana!

Children also communicate through their visual art. Their drawings and paintings can indicate understanding of specific concepts. Even so, every child has individual abilities and styles that are open to interpretation.

Just as other parents do, I collected and dated my young daughters' artwork, and noticed some differences between them. They chose to depict different subjects; they had different styles; and they used differing amounts of detail in their artwork.

As adults, however, both my daughters appreciate many examples of art, and both of them love to design and create a variety of artistic products. Linnet, my oldest, invents striking interior environments and paints colorful murals. My daughter Julia, six years younger, knits complex sweaters and scarves, and composes music with lyrics.

Adults won't typecast a person based only on a few examples of childhood art. As all children grow, they change their preferences, improve their skills, and develop new talents.

Of course, they still CAN'T WAIT TO COMMUNICATE!

# BIBLIOGRAPHY

Berk, L. E. (2013) Child Development, 9th Edition. London, UK: Pearson Education

Buckley, B. (2003) Children's Communication Skills: From birth to five years. New York, NY: Routledge, Taylor & Francis Group

Carson, J. (1997) Tell Me About Your Picture: Art Activities to Help Children Communicate. Upper Saddle River, NJ: Dale Seymour

Corke, M. (2012) Using Playful Practice to Communicate with Special Children. London, UK: Taylor & Francis Ltd

Davies-Arai, S. (2015) Communicating with Kids: What Works and What Doesn't. Leicester, UK: Matador Publishing

Devine, A. (2015) Literacy for Visual Learners: Teaching Children with Learning Differences to Read, Write, Communicate and Create. Philadelphia, PA: Jessica Kingsley Publishers

Elgin, S. H. (1996) The Gentle Art of Communicating with Kids. Hoboken, NJ: John Wiley & Sons, Inc.

Gerber, M. (1998) Dear Parent (Caring for Infants with Respect) Los Angeles, CA: Resources for Infant Educarers

Gerber, M. and Johnson, A. (1997) Your Self-Confident Baby: How to Encourage Your Child's Natural Abilities - From the Very Start. Hoboken, NJ: John Wiley & Sons, Inc.

Gopnik, A. (2016) The Gardener and the Carpenter: What the New Science of Child Development Tells Us about the Relationship Between Parents and Children. New York: Farrar, Straus & Giroux

Kimell, S. (2018) How to Talk So Children Will Listen & Learn: How to Communicate with Your Child to Build a Trustworthy Relationship, Engage Cooperation, Set Limits, and Prevent Conflicts. Scotts Valley, CA: CreateSpace Independent Publishing

Manolson, A. (1992) It Takes Two to Talk: A Parent's Guidebook to Helping Children Communicate. Toronto, CAN: The Hanen Centre

McKinnon, E. (1997) Ready to Communicate: Enhancing Your Child's Verbal Skills. Waldoboro, ME: Totline Publications

Mountrose, P. (1999) Tips and Tools for Getting Thru to Kids: 25 Great Ways to Communicate with Children & Teens. London, UK: Holistic Communications

Sull, T. (2004) Can't Wait to Communicate From Birth to Four. Chapel Hill, NC: Professional Press

Ward, S. (2001) Babytalk: Strengthen Your Child's Ability to Listen, Understand, and Communicate. New York, NY: Ballantine Books

# FOR TAKING NOTES

Page/Paragraph _____

_____

_____

_____

_____

_____

_____

_____

_____

_____

_____

_____

_____

_____

# FOR TAKING NOTES

Page/Paragraph _____

_____

_____

_____

_____

_____

_____

_____

_____

_____

_____

_____

_____

_____

_____

# EXAM QUESTIONS

CHAPTER I         Discuss a basic concept of literacy.
                  Discuss self-empowerment in communication.

CHAPTER II        Define Receptive and Expressive language
                  Define Nature and Nurture.

CHAPTER III       Describe adults' body language to use with
                  toddlers.
                  Discuss Reflective Listening.

CHAPTER IV        Describe three ways to give experiences with books.
                  Which picture books would you read aloud,
                  and why?

CHAPTER V         How can preschoolers learn about the alphabet?
                  Discuss Circle Games for young children.

CHAPTER VI        Discuss Friedrich Froebel and kindergarten.
                  What is a Speakers Circle? Why is it valuable?

CHAPTER VII       Name and describe three Writing Exercises.
                  Describe a child's autobiography.

CPSIA information can be obtained
at www.ICGtesting.com
Printed in the USA
LVHW040212280519
619246LV00002B/349/P

9 781950 540983